Wrinkles;

FROM THE

BROW OF EXPERIENCE,

And Other Poems.

BY

JAMES WOODMANSEE,

Author of "The Closing Scene."

Cincinnati:

1860.

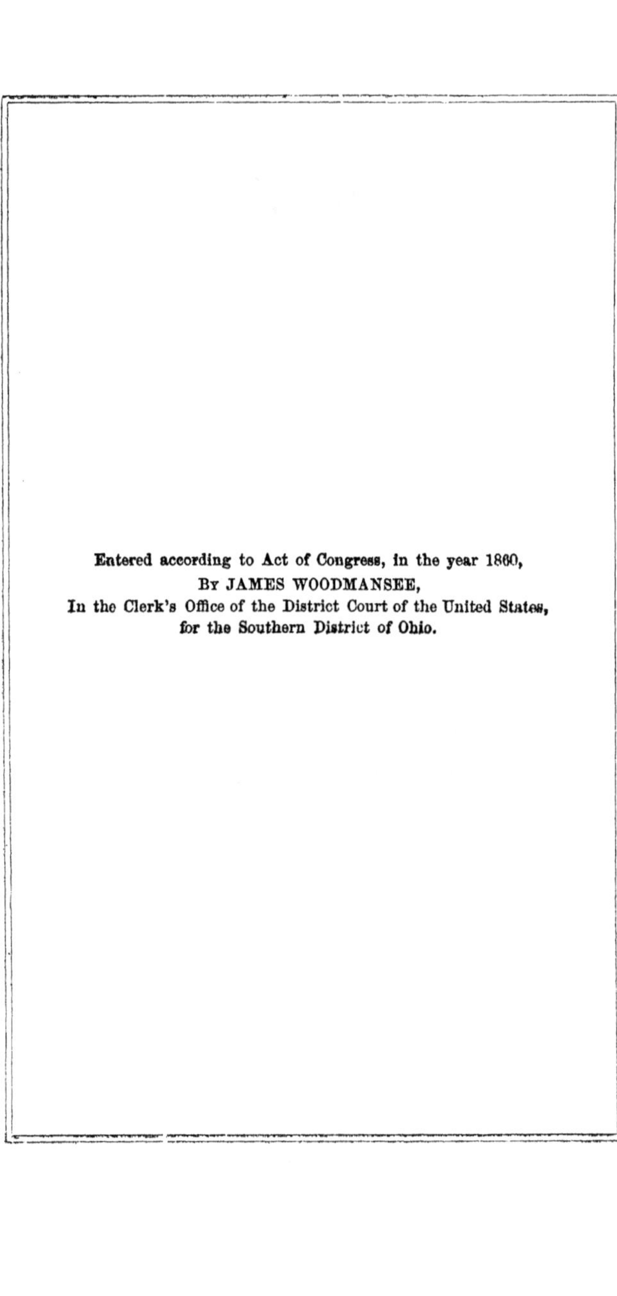

Entered according to Act of Congress, in the year 1860,
By JAMES WOODMANSEE,
In the Clerk's Office of the District Court of the United States,
for the Southern District of Ohio.

Preface.

There are no richer treasures to be bought,
Than living Maxims, sparkling, deathless Thought.

SUGAR VALLEY, A. D. 1860.

Dedication to Wisdom.

I hope I've pluck'd without offense
From brow of sage Experience,
These WRINKLES quaint—the laws of Fate!
Which I, O, WISDOM! DEDICATE
To you, who unto others do
All that you'd have them do to you.

Proem.

Poor Human Nature is a book—huge Book!
As broad and mighty are its pages all,
As vast, well-deep the wisdom it contains,—
Frail Nature's Book of Follies without end!

This book is ope to every eye of man;
But men have met me in the walks of life
Who have made Art and Science all their own,
And think themselves the Magi of the world,
That scarcely read its Preface while they live!
Sage Wisdom's babes shall grow up Folly's men,
When, with a bat-like blindness of the soul,
They will not see a mid-day sun that shines
To turn their night of Nature into day,—
Poor Human Nature's Bible will not read—
That book of frailties by Human Nature
Penn'd out and printed plain upon all flesh;
A revelation, truthfully revealing
To man, that night of all enigmas—MAN!
We must look into *self* to—*know ourselves;*
This one truth missed, what is there else to know
Save God, and nothingness of all beside?
For this, our mother Eve all Eden gave,
And her bright crown of Immortality.
Men that eat up this book, alone are wise;

Ay, Wisdom's self was but a child, till his
Far-seeing eye and hungry soul devour'd
Its every page, and made them all his own:
And man ne'er was, nor will, nor can be great,
Tho' his name's echo talks from college halls,
Till FINIS of this book is his A. M.

Mankind, to know mankind, must study—Man;
The world's profoundly wise do study deepest
Poor Human Nature's Book of Frailties,—
Encyclopedia of all science—truth!
The fabled stone that turns all dross to gold!
The rod of Moses and water's gush!
The wand that breaks the spell of all enchantments
And turns man's *minus* into *plus* at will!
The Alpha, Omega of earthly books—
The A B C of the great book of Life,
That makes us cry EUREKA, while we live!
Ay, here the key of all our knowledge lies,—
'Tis Learning's crown and Wisdom's utmost bound;
Boundary that human genius may not pass—
Third heaven and home to wing of glorious mind,—
The all on this side—mortal, beyond—God!

Man! study Human Nature and be wise;
Heaven-eyed Philosophy, more riches here
May find, than hunting new worlds 'mong the stars;
It teacheth *self!* bless'd lesson known by few.
Must know thyself e'er thou canst govern self:—
This *self* is eel-like in its slipperiness,

And would not be examined by daylight;
Man seeks for wisdom—all, but—*know himself*,—
In science colleged, ignorant in *self*
Are those that this world's tongue pronounces *wise*:—
Great lesson this—*to know we nothing know*.

This book's wide ope to every eye,—read—read!
Tho' imperfection blots its every page
And cries—'Behold an imperfection perfect,'
'T is Life's school book and Time's philosophy;
A text-book for the deeply-thinking wise;
'Tis Reason's rule—'tis Science's highest school
That maketh men true graduates indeed;
Light of Experience, and Wisdom's all,—
Nay, wisdom's not Wisdom, till patient hand
Hath turned with care its sacred pages o'er,
And learnt this truth—a lesson quite divine:
'*To know himself*,'—the all that man can know.

That book is—Man! revealing man to man.
Man! read man like a book, and 'KNOW THYSELF,"
And thou hast learned the alphabet of Heaven.

Experience.

Experience is a hoary-headed Sage,
With hairy cheek and winter-bearded chin,
And his face maps out Old Antiquity
Plain as the dial's shade the hours of day.
Experience, too, hath sacred Wisdom's head,
Attention's smallest-whisper-hearing ear,
Persuasion's tongue of dropping eloquence,
And Penetration's eye that sees things as they are:
Yea, his all-seeing eye scans ghostly Past,
Looks on thro' heart down to the soul of things,
And e'en in Wisdom's head finds vacuum!
He 's one who looks 'round other ends of times,
And sees upon both sides of things at once,—
Beholds the years in womb of Embryo,
And reads '*to come*,' as it will be when born;
By ruined Past the living Present views,
And eyelays ghost of blank Futurity.

He is the mirror of Intelligence,
Time's open book and Life's philosophy
Sent to dispel the night of Ignorance:—
Poor Human Nature sheds her robe of dust—
Revealed, and bare, and naked, to his sight!
His precepts all are pearls of priceless price,
And those who scorn them are base Folly's fools—

In knowledge all unschool'd, and in themselves,
And they shall learn wise lessons from his lash.
He teacheth Folly wisdom, and unscales
The eyes of those that would of choice be blind,—
Compels e'en Blindness' self to learn of him!
Tho' fool's back oft his iron rod rends sore,
Yet every lash that falls is for his good,—
A weight of knowledge gives not else obtained.
He is as Mercy's self, and spares the rod
Till Folly 'side from own true interest turns:—
Within the school of sage Experience,
E'en Folly learns—*in future to be wise.*

He 's Nature's teacher, training the untrained
Life's devious paths to run and stumble not,—
To steer Man's bark o'er Time's tumultuous sea
To harbor safe of Happiness and Heaven.
He wears a world of things in his long head—
Strength-intellectual strong as pyramid!
Each Wrinkle of his Brow, wise lesson is
To Wisdom's self, not found in all the books;
And one by one, I pluck them off at will,
To gem the crown on Wisdom's hoary brow.

Wrinkles,

FROM THE

BROW OF EXPERIENCE.

WRINKLE I.

Look into self, and seek thyself to know,—
Knowledge enough to understand below.

II.

Wouldst thou learn much, learn little at a time,
Add Perseverance, and the crown is thine.

III.

On with Ambition
To gain addition
To—Reputation.

IV.

Souls, subject unto *dust*, are slaves;
Men that subdue not *self* are knaves,—
Must *conquer*, to be good and great,
And labor, if you'd fill your pate :—
Burst spirit-bonds—self-victors be,
Soul-freedom is—heaven-liberty.

V.

If you to Fortune would aspire,
Fling all your irons in the fire,
And blow and strike, and—*never tire.*

VI.

Sap-headed Folly cries—'I *could* do,'
Arm-folded Indolence—'I *will* do,'
While Wisdom's actions speak—'*I do do.*'

WISDOM.

WRINKLE I.

The spirit's heavenly light
A-shine on Mental night.

II.

True Wisdom's guide is Reason's rules,
While sad Experience is the fool's.

III.

Sage Wisdom! mid-day's sun—Mind-life and light,
Whose floods of glory chase dark Error's night.

IV.

Blest Wisdom freights life's moment ere it flies
With Virtue's diamonds, loaded for the skies;
But Foolery grins to Foolery as she goes
To home of horrors, and to world of woes.

FOLLY.

WRINKLE I.

The child of Chaos and Eternal Night,
Not born to life by brooding Spirit's light.

II.

From Wisdom's Eden-path base Folly flies,
Shadows to find, and loose realities.

III.

The fool buys wisdom at his folly's cost,
And all he knows is learnt from what he's lost.

IV.

Starv'd fools oft live and die in hope
Of cast-off gown, or petticoat.

V.

Her owlet-eyes, dim at the light,
And only gaze upon the night.

VI.

The blindest bat on earth is she,
Who having eyes—*she will not see.*

VII.

She heaps God-daring mountains to the sky,
And they shall fall upon her by and by;
She is forever like the lightning-rod,
Aspiring heaven to feel the bolts of God.

FASHION.

WRINKLE I.

The scholar of vain Fashion's school
Learns first to be base Folly's tool,
Then graduates—*Time's silly fool*—
To toe the mark of Vanity by rule.

VANITY.

WRINKLE I.

When e'er I see a gilded form,
Or walking thing of pride,
I'm always sure their richest coat
Is on their outward side.

AMBITION.

WRINKLE I.

Greatness, in travail for a greater name,
Mortal, upreaching for immortal Fame.

II.

The shrub, low-bending in the vale,
Doth play securely with the gale,
Whiles lo! the lofty mountain oak
Down falls—smote with the thunder's stroke.

RENOWN.

WRINKLE I.

Renown is, Life's own true sublime,
Soul's foot-prints left in sands of Time.

II.

The sea-shell whispers on for aye
Of worth it once possess'd;
So doth Renown perfume the name
Of Fame's departed bless'd.

POET.

WRINKLE I.

In temple high of Fame
The Poet carves his name,
The glory of his nation
Till Time's desolation.

LEARNING.

WRINKLE I.

To mental-night
Gives spirit-light,—
Lights Wisdom's lamp to show
Mysteries in embryo.

TONGUE.

WRINKLE I.

Do not our *two* ears and *one* tongue proclaim,
Hear *twice*, and speak but *once*, or come to shame?

II.

Without leg-traveling goes pell-mell,
And flies without a wing,—
Iniquity on fire of hell,
And deadly is its sting.

PREJUDICE.

WRINKLE I.

His bat-like vision blinds at noonday light,
But looks owl-like into the heart of night.

II.

He shuts his lids and bars out light,
Like somber owl in hollow tree,
And makes his own bat-eyes of night
Worse than stone-blind—*they will not see!*

MISER.

WRINKLE I.

Gaping and all athirst for gain,
Like the parch'd earth for summer's rain.

II.

To-morrow, is the day when Misers give,
When Vice reforms, Sloth works, and—*dead men live!*

HUMAN NATURE.

WRINKLE I.

A wretched Feebleness by Sin debased
Is Human Nature, till remade by Grace.

II.

Life's page is dark with Imperfection's dots,
And often black, alas! with Error's blots.

III.

Man, with Perfection, is not bless'd,—
The Rose, with every beauty dress'd,
Is queen of Flowers—the Garden's gem,
But, many thorns are on her stem!

2

SIN.

WRINKLE I.

Perversity all o'er,
Corruption to the core:—
A sinner hugging Sin
Makes all the Devils grin!

VIRTUE.

WRINKLE I.

The Sun's blown out by wing of Night,
And Moon eclips'd by Morning's light;
But, *Virtue* shines divinely fair,
Forever fix'd—the glittering Bear.

II.

To give her back to man, the Savior died,
And wealth of Worlds is nothing by her side.

III.

The oned with Virtue, are divinely bless'd,—
Be found of her, and God will do the rest.

IV.

Illume Life's path with Virtue's heavenly day,
And you'll not stumble in the Narrow-way.

NEW BIRTH.

WRINKLE I.

The soul, by New-birth woke from Carnal-night,
Is all alive with Spirit-life—*God-light!*

II.

When Spirit's glories day the heart of night,
Soul wakes up Eden! born to life and light.

III.

Not all the diamond-crowns by Monarchs wore,
Or all the pearl upon the ocean's shore;
Nor all the gold of Ophir and Peru,—
Ay, all the wealth this mundane Earth e'er knew,
Can make me rich as that poor beggar is
That's made Heaven's gem divine—***Religion*** his.

IV.

Religion is the soul's new birth,
And its celestial day,—
The spirit's comforter and guide.
Life's heavenly ecstacy.

CHRISTIAN.

WRINKLE I.

His Heaven-oped eye looks upward to his God,
And cleaves to Him tho' smitten with the rod.

CONSCIENCE.

WRINKLE I.

Let Conscience keep her mirror bright
Illumed by Virtue's heavenly light,
That Soul may see herself within
Reflecting God—unmar'd by Sin.

TEMPERANCE.

WRINKLE I.

Blest Temp'rance lengthens out our day,
And makes Life's close—Time's own decay.

II.

Health, Wisdom, in dry regions live,
And drink their brandy from a sieve.

MAN.

WRINKLE I.

Man, enters into life—crying,
Travels sorely through it—sighing,
And ends it with a groan—dying.

II.

'Frail Man,' 't is said, 'is nothing but a worm;'
Then—*one that hath full many ways to squirm!*

III.

Treads Duty's path slow-crawling as the snail,
But flies in Crime's like vessel under sail.

IV.

Man buys his bread with toil and tears,
And trusts his God with doubts and fears.

V.

Man oft builds Babel to defy his God,
Till Satan-like he falls—smote with the rod.

VI.

Frail Man! O, let him crawl in dust—
And tortoise-like, or fall he must.

VII.

Man is afloat on Time's death-raging sea
Where every wave he meets is—destiny.

VIII.

Man's *hopes* are dogged by doubts and fears,
Well as his *love*, by groans and tears.

IX.

Man leaves Life's banquet with a sigh,
To fast with dread—Eternity.

WOMAN.

WRINKLE I.

There is a magnet in fair Woman's charms
That draw'th e'en sacred Wisdom to her arms!
And there is loadstone too, within her smiles,
That siren-like bewitches and beguiles.

II.

God-sends, and Beauty-flowerets from above,
To be entwined with men—garlands of Love!

III.

The center, being, soul, and crown of all
God's works,—perfection and the end of all.

LOVE.

WRINKLE I.

Love twines vine-like around the human heart,
Of Man's existence to become a part.

II.

To this great maxim let the World agree,
And—'LOVE FOREVER,' let the adage be.

MARRIAGE.

WRINKLE I.

Two hearts link'd! *one* in trouble
To make life's pleasures—*double*:—
Twain, mingled to a perfect *one*
To make a heavenly unison.

II.

Soul clave to soul—
Magnet and pole!

III.

Heaven-bless'd-heart-union, and the bosom's peace,—
The Life of Love, and a perpetual feast:—
Such hearts have found their homes, and Passions rest,
By laws of Nature, and by Union bless'd.

IV.

If Happiness is found beneath the sun,
'T is owned by *twain* united into *one*,—
Earth's all is found,—a Paradise below,
And all Time's pleasures in this Eden flow.

LIFE.

WRINKLE I.

Life, is—soul-salt that saves
Mortality from graves.

II.

Life seems composed of—partings—meetings,
And sighings—snarlings—empty greetings.

III.

Life's history:—Births, deaths of friends and foes,
Man's chase around the world—*after his nose!*

IV.

Frail Mortals live, and then—away to God,
And they do leave behind—the path they trod.

V.

Perplexing maze of care and pain—
Black Error and Affliction's reign.

VI.

Life gives to mortals all,
The wormwood and the gall,
From cradle to the pall.

VII.

Our Life is frail,—a rose-wreath'd bower
That often withers in an hour.

VIII.

We live to spin Life's brittle thread,
Draw out—and snap, and we are—dead!

IX.

Roses of health to-day we bloom,
To-morrow—gathered to the tomb!

X.

Life, is a lamp, that wastes its fires
Both night and day, till it expires.

XI.

Life, is a race,—so fleetly it is run—
A moment past, goal 's reach'd and laurel 's won!

XII.

Our life, is like an empty bubble
Upon Time's tempest-billow, trouble,
To flit one moment o'er the sea
And burst, and all 's—Eternity

XIII.

Dead! and forgotten
E'er we be rotten!

XIV.

We live—we die! and all in vain
Unless it be—*to live again.*

DEATH.

WRINKLE I.

Life-clock's last click! The boundary line
Between Eternity and Time.

II.

Death is the point—the close
Of Life's cares all and woes.

III.

Death's hand 's congenial to our suffering clay,
And makes it sleep without a pang for aye.

IV.

Death's coming sets the spirit free,
And wakes to—Immortality.

V.

The only wealth complete,
Lies in our—winding-sheet.

THE GRAVE.

WRINKLE I.

The Grave 's the clay-house for our clay,
And entrance to—Eternal Day.

II.

The smiles of Heaven illume
The dark night of the tomb.

III.

There is but one thing certain 'neath the sun—
A *Grave*,—and that, poor Mortals, fain would shun!

THE BODY.

WRINKLE I.

The Body, is Soul's prison-house of clay,—
A shadow, flitting from the smile of day:
Autumnal-landscapes' Eden-painted smiles,
When icy Winter comes, are turned to wilds,—
So, Soul's frail tenement! its Life-god fled,
It fades—pales—falls to dust; and Man is—*dead.*

ETERNITY.

WRINKLE I

A shoreless sea—
Eternity!

II.

So many leaves, fan not the summer-hours,
Nor Earth's green bosom nest so many flowers,—
Grass-spears so many in fields, wolds and woods,—
So many waves, ne'er danc'd Old Ocean's floods,
Nor do so many sands shore every sea,
As there are *years*, in vast Eternity.

MISCELLANEOUS.

WRINKLE I.

Life, is—bright moments, gloomy hours;
Earth,—shadows, shades, sunshine and showers.

II.

Earth's grain of wheat, and peck of tares,
Man stores by toil, and turns to—tears.

III.

This Earth, is but a hollow globe
For all to ring, and see
What Solomon sighed out to find—
An empty vanity.

IV.

Vain Cowards talk e'er Battle is begun,
But Heroes triumph, after victories won.

V.

A loving Saviour useth clay
As He used it in ancient day,—
To bless with sight—*eye of the blind*,
And open Eden to mankind.

VI.

Our life-thoughts all, should be God-worshipers
Tho' groaning 'neath Affliction's rod,
And Being's stream flow unpolluted on
Till mingled with its Fountain—God.

FINAL.

On Eyebrow of Experience
All wrinkles now I see;
For Folly, each wears all its frowns,
But Wisdom! none for thee.

TO CRITICS.

Now, Critic! to all others do
As you would have them do to you:—
Obey the Saviour's golden rule,
And not be adaged for a fool.

THE CHRISTIAN.

The Christian.

The happy Christian now my pencil paints;
Let Earth behold Heaven's likness of a man
In whom unites all earthly excellence—
By excellence adorn'd and manly grace,—
With every grace and virtue heavenly fair,
By Earth and Heaven, by Angels loved, and God.

The man that doth deserve the name of *Man*,
E'en he whom his Creator made upright
And in his nostrils breath'd immortal soul,—
The handiwork and image of his God
Arm'd with that panoply of Heaven—*pure heart!*
His heart's the home of the bless'd Comforter,
A sacred temple consecrate to God—
Heart-wed to God as needle to its pole!
His soul's a casket rich with every gem
That's worth the seeking this side Paradise;
His brow wears frowns for Folly, Sin and Crime;
His eye is single, and is full of light—
Heaven in his eye and God in all his thoughts.
Wisdom, from tongue of truth, as manna falls,
And he alone hath heavenly knowledge found—
Sage Wisdom's light—*he hath with Jesus been*,
And name of Jesus is his forehead's crown.
He's knowledge-wise above frail Learning's art,

A graduate in Virtue's heavenly school,—
Hath pull'd off Nature's rags and put on Christ,
And Virtue's robes celestial beauty give—
Religion's graces wears and finds them heaven!
The child of Grace, with good Desires awake
And Passions quell'd and conquer'd and enchain'd,
Emptied of Carnal Mind and born again,—
Right onward to Perfection pressing still
Till *will* is lost—so mingled with the Lord's
He doth the will of God—*doing his own*—
Doing His will as Angels in the Heavens!
To see the Christian is to love the saint,
And more we know, the lovelier he appears—
A loveliness that loveth all mankind!
He's serious, not sad; cheerful, not gay;
Sedate, demure—an Israelite indeed.
To spirit-light and life his all is wed:
His every pleasure is in Righteousness,
And his rejoicing in Perfection is,—
Day-bright in faith and in all hope made glad.
His looks announce to all:—'*There is a God
And this the copy!*'—Heaven is seen in him!
All eyes behold—Tranquillity and Peace—
Sweet Peace within and Virtue's reign supreme,—
A soul all Edened with the smiles of Heaven.
He is the likeness of the Deity,—
God sees himself in every holy man—
Almighty-shadow, visible to men!

In all things he begins and ends with God,
And high-exalted holds God in full view,
Obliterating all save only God—
His All in All and wherewithall for aye.
He lives so near to Son of Righteousness
Soul drinks eternal-day from His bright beams,
And finds in Him there's fullness evermore.
He feels and knows he is the Lord's redeem'd;
Experience past and present feelings speak
Religion true and no delusion is—
Soul-joy supreme and spiritual delight,
And where she is, there is, there must be—heaven,
And his full soul rejoices in its strength:
The Christian leaps for joy at present bliss,
What will he do when Heaven opes—*all his own?*
Religion plants a little heaven in breast—
A little heaven is every holy heart!
His present life's a life of cheerfulness,
And life to come—eternal joy and peace.
Religion is his life's bright ornament,
Gives Pleasure's plume to fleeting wing of Time—
Perfume and luster to his memory.
He is the happy man, Truth's tongue declares,
Forever happy, 'cause forever good—
With all Religion's glories in his heart,
And hath a heaven to go to Heaven in!
Where'er he is, is happiness and joy,
Whither he goes are pleasures evermore—
His life's cup runneth over with delight,—

O! what a heaven there is in being good!
To live is pleasure and to die is gain,—
His dreams by night, an open'd Paradise!

He stands with *Meekness*, looking love to man,
Cloth'd with Humility as with a robe,
And ever found close to the cross of Christ;
He's Meekness self reveal'd in human form,
Where Christ exalted is, and self abased,
In his eyes nothing—greatness in his God's:
Meek, humble, tho' son, heir of the Most High,—
A spirit-meekness poor as Poverty,
But rich in faith—rejoicing in the Lord.
A *Pilgrim*, journeying to Promised Land,
One lost in mighty wilderness of Time,
And his inquiry: '*Where 's my Father's house?*'
Whilst traveling on to Zion's holy hill.
He eyes not present, but his future home,
Blind to this world, and all awake to next,
With less of fortune here, than treasure there.
Content with little, satisfied with less,
And walks with bless'd Contentment on life's day,
And richer, happier beyond compare
Than king who calls the Universe his own.
He lets the world go by, and knows it dust,
And thro' its emptiness, God's fullness sees—
Emptied of Earth and fill'd with Heaven entire!
He hath abandon'd Earth, and idols all,
In Virtue's flowery paths to walk with Peace,
And find the Narrow-way leads straight to Life.

Converses more with God than with mankind—
In sweet communion with the Lord of all!
His mind's above corroding cares of Time,
God, and not Mammon, dwells within his heart;
Dead to the world, and lives to Heaven alone—
God in his thoughts and Earth beneath his feet—
Earth 'neath his feet and God alone above!
His heart, the altar is of Prayer and Praise,
And incense ever smokes therefrom to Heaven;
His soul, like Angel's harp harmonious strung
To hymn hosannas to the Lord of Hosts:
Devotion's fiery chariot mounts the skies,
While every heart-string like a Seraph's lyre
Psalms out to God soul-adoration pure—
His God-fill'd life devoted to his God.
His being is one song of thankfulness,
Thankful for winter's cold as summer's heat;
Each moment plumes Devotion's wing for Heaven,
Each breath he breathes one voiceless prayer to God,
And ceaseless praise for ceaseless mercies gives;
Nor longer wishes he to breathe on Earth
Than soul breathes psalms of love to Lord of Life
On pealing to the ear of Deity.
And heavenly manna in abundance feeds
His heaven-wed soul through wilderness of life
Till heart shouts out '*A loving Savior near!*'
And finds his Paradise in being good.

His life is one long walk with *Charity*—
A charity that loveth friends and foes,

And thinks of injuries only to forgive,—
He hath no eye to see his brother's faults,
But he hath two, to gaze upon his good.
At others' griefs, his heart knows how to melt,
A friend to bless'd Humanity and Man:—
Lives not for self, but good of all mankind,
For God did make them all, and bid him love,—
Loves, that—some heirs of Glory he may love.
Where Duty calls, he goes with Peace along,
And Want and Poverty forget their wants;
His ear is ope to groan of Wretchedness,
And both hands ready to relieve Distress;
Hears Suffering's cries, and all his answers bless,—
The good Samaritan that brings Relief—
God-bless'd, that he to man might blessings be!

His being is a brilliant, burning *zeal*,
A burning zeal to do his Father's will—
A living coal from altar of the Lord.
He's steadfast as fix'd star in heavenly orb,
And all unwavering as the sun in heaven—
A martyr-perseverance until death.
Fears naught but God, and hates but Sin alone,
And dares do right, tho' Death and Hell oppose!
He is the zeal that lion's den can't daunt,
Or seven-times-heated furnace make afraid.
The Christian's race is not for purse of gold,
But weight of Glory,—*zealous let him be.*
Not to be zealous is impiety;
Not to be diligent, mockery to God,—
To act the sluggard is to damn the soul.

He fights, not to lay cities desolate,
But warfare is to take high Heaven by storm,
Then, should he sleep as having naught to do?
Ah! less than zealous, speaks a coward wretch,
And less than ardor, traitor and—Judas!
His life's all ardor—not to please the world,
But meet the approbation of the Judge;
He's ever valiant in true Valor's cause,
And ever conquers, tho' he wars with Hell.
Seek for, and find the Christian at his post,
Forever found where heavenly manna falls,
In labors sweet of Piety and love:—
Ne'er out of place, but ever in the right;
With his oil-filled and brightly-burning lamp
He tends to Angel-duties of the church,—
To duties true as sun to zodiac—
A pillar strong in temple of his God!
The cross is not a burden, but his crown,
To do his duty, is his heart's delight:
Joy, to the Christian's soul, known Duty is,
Her angel-finger to Devotion points,—
With wing'd Delight to every duty flies
Conversing with the Savior face to face!
In heavenly places sips of Jesus' love
And Edens life in service of his God—
A joy divine beyond the halls of Mirth.
Truth's mirror bright reflecting much of Heaven,
Where Christ and bless'd Religion are reveal'd—
An earthly constellation bright with God,
Salvation's heir array'd by Righteousness,

Elect and precious—chosen of the Lord.

That man lives best, and most to purpose lives
Who makes Religion's graces all his own;
That man to purpose lives who lives to die,
And he is rich who makes sweet Heaven his own.
I love the man that bows and honors God—
The holy Christian loved by Savior's love,
My friend—the first on Memory's sacred desk,
For he's the *Perfect* man—the man of Uz!
Alive to Virtue, 'wake to every good,—
Doth all the good he can to friend and foe,
And gems life's crown with heavenly Virtues all,
And loves his God 'bove all things else beside:—
Good-deeds, do track his path of life as thick
And bright, as Milky-way the firmament.
He useth time, to get well out of time,
And lives to die, and dies to live again;
He in his Bible lives—the light of Earth!
His meat and drink to do his Father's will.
Life's study is to weed life of its tares,
Have all pure wheat fit for the garner's use;
His only care, to plant stars in his crown,
And store his treasures safe in house of God:—
He stores Heaven-treasure as a miser gold,
And gems each minute as it flies with Praise,—
Crowds in each moment what is worth all worlds
And lays up wealth enough in time's short day
To life his immortality with Heaven.
His school is Virtue, and preceptor Christ—

Right onward to Perfection in His steps,
In all the gospel armor clad complete,
With good o'ercoming Evil evermore,—
Fulfilling law—'gainst such there is no law!
He walks on Earth, yet lives above the world;
There is much less of Earth in him than Heaven,—
So much of Heaven he seems not made of dust,
Divorc'd from Earth and wholly wed to God—
As near like God as flesh and blood can be!
He's lost to self, and God his All in All,
Quite dead to Sin, and lives to God alone—
So near like Christ that God is visible!
Life, one continued scene of Holiness—
God-light, day-gleaming to the world around!
His being, is a chart of Piety,
His life, a written book for all to read,—
Heaven's copy fair of what a Man should be:
The Christian's pattern and the child of Heaven,
God-loving and Sin-daring man of Christ
Whose soul is one bright heaven of Deity
Wherein the Holy Spirit loves to dwell.

Could I but half his greatness sing, you'd say:
''Tis not Truth's harp, but Flattery's that sings.'
He is the man for Earth and also Heaven,
He lives the praise and glory of both worlds,—
Uniting all of Earthly excellence
With heavenly Virtues all—*met in one man.*
A man for Angels to admire and love;
The praise, delight and wonder of his kind;

Earth's ornament and glory of the world;
And he alone hath title to the skies—
Perfection walking up to Paradise!
The only man that answers life's great end;
The only man that to full stature grows,
Where image of the Deity is seen—
A Samson 'mong Philistines of Earth!
He, 'lone hath the eternal Wisdom found,—
The wisest that All-seeing Eye beholds—
Earth's all that Deity beholds and loves.
To him, Religion, heavenly knowledge gives
And opes the fountain of eternal Day,—
Perfection by Religion perfected!
Philosophy, thro' telescope views stars;
His eye sees clear where optic-tubes grow dim—
Faith-eyed beholds a Paradise beyond:
How high Religion can exalt a man!
Celestial heights above his fellow men
Tho' they are kings, and he a beggar is,—
Exalteth e'en to Heaven, a—Lazarus!
Above the world while walking on the Earth—
In God, whiles he is towering 'mong mankind—
A son of God, joint heir with Jesus Christ!
'Yond titles great—renown beyond Renown,
Divinely beautiful with Holiness—
Of such are white-robed saints that shout 'round God.
Of God's own handi-work, the end and crown,
The noblest work that Deity hath wrought—
A likeness true of his eternal Sire.
God's Bride, with whom the Savior is in love—

All that keeps Earth from sinking down to Hell;
Would Sin-cursed Earth without him live an hour?
Nay, it had wreck'd six thousand years ago.
The chosen Christian doth unite the smile
Of great Omnipotence to Being's soul,
Else, a chaotic emptiness and hell,—
Love that unites Creation to its God—
A wonder 'proaching near a miracle!
For the Elect's sake all things do exist:—
For him, sweet Mercy wears her smile of heaven;
For him, was many-mansion'd Heaven prepar'd;
Life's tree planted; Eternal rest allowed;
Bright Glory offer'd free to sons of men;
God's Blessedness made ready to receive,
And Juda's Lion oped the seal'd-up book
In presence-chamber of the great I AM.
He is his country's friend, his own and Heaven's;
His friends are Virtue's, and his foes are God's,
All Virtues reign in Eden of his soul—
An Eden-lily blossoming below
To beautify Earth's barrenness and curse!
A rose immortal budding upon Earth
To bloom for aye in garden of his God!
A tree of Life in vineyard of the Lord
So prun'd and water'd by the Husbandman
That it produces fruit an hundred fold
To fill the storehouse of Omnipotence.

He keeps his coffin in his eye thro' life,
And makes grim Death familiar as a friend.

Life with Religion crown'd, uncrowneth Death.
His *death-bed scene*, speaks out Religion's worth,—
DEATH-BED! A holy place,—how near it stands
To God! 'Tis on the very verge of Heaven!
Pause solemn 'twixt Eternity and Time
Where Vanity is Vanity no more.
It is the school of Wisdom to the wise,
Where Death's white face looks from its shroud on Life,
Declaring loud:—'YOU SOON SHALL BE AS I,'—
Death-knell that makes creation stand aghast!
The bed, where Life is born—Eternal Life;
The golden autumn, crowning Life's whole year;
The last kind *inn*, on our short journey home,
And soul and body's 'FAREWELL,' until Morn.

He's full of days, and satisfied with life—
Willing to live, and willing, too, to die,
And back to God smile his pure soul away,—
To live is Christ, to die—eternal gain.
His work is finish'd when his Savior calls,
And like Elijah waits the car of fire
To mount in flaming chariot to God
And blaze in splendor like a mid-day sun.
Life's well-spent day crowns dying couch with joys
As thick as stars in galaxy of heaven,
And not a stain his spirit-robe defiles—
More fit for Heaven than for a sinful world.

He is a traveler thro' the Shades of Death
To God's bright city—e'en his Father's house!

To brink of Jordan, Christian now arrives
A-lean upon the staff of his Beloved,
And shouts to see the Passover at hand—
E'er ready to depart and be with God.
He lived to die—now dies to live again,—
To lay that throbbing mass of anguish by
And put the deathless robe of Glory on,—
Lose dust, to find bright Immortality,—
Let Adam fall, and new man speed to God!
To Father's bosom not afraid to go,—
Why should he fear to meet Death's dart, and fall?
Where is his home? Heaven. And his portion who?
God—his eternal crown, immense reward!
Tears, groans of Earth, for joys immortal give!
Well may he shout, firm stand on brink of death
And Victory claim e'en in the battle's heat.
Death's door unlock'd, he wakes in Jesus' arms,
Soul plumes her wings for Incorruption's home
To hold companionship with sainted ones—
To all that's lovely, think of what you will;
O'er thrones and kingdoms to be crown'd of God,
An heir of Heaven and Immortality.
There is no Hell 'twixt Faithfulness and God;
The Vale and Shade of Death, is but a *shade*
Where Spirit finds eternal Liberty;
Life-stop, where soul awaits to be refresh'd
E'er she beholds her Savior face to face:
The Mount Immortal towers above Death Vale,
And light of life extends to smile of God.
A holy place the Christian's death-bed is—

The softest down man ever slept upon!
Where Jesus smiles, can there be aught of ill?
Stern Death's approach is Glory drawing near.
His friends all gather round the dying man
To see the exit of a sinless soul,—
With Nature's suffering clay to sympathize,
Whiles spirit gives its earth to Earth again
To fill the law, and satisfy the tomb.
Serene he smiles at Death's insidious dart,
Frail Nature's prison-house to desolate,—
To make the Heaven-born captive, Spirit all,
And dying couch, the—*Paradise of Death.*

On Nebo's mount he views bright Canaan near,
And soul communes with God:—'I'm almost home!
A few steps more, I'm at my Father's house,—
Reveal thy glories, Heaven! and shorten time.
I would awake from Time's deep sleep, O Lord!
And rise from tent of death to be with Thee:
I'm waiting to depart to be with Christ
My day in night of death and strength in dust!
Upon night-side of Jordan now I stand,—
Divide the waters, Lord! and let me pass.'

The Christian ceas'd, and deep in spirit groan'd,—
Soul, struggles with its dust to be a god!
The life-stream curdles and the death-dews start,—
Each pain shall give him weight of blessedness!
Frail Nature's bark's nigh wreck'd in Gulf of Death,
But Spirit plumes for haven of Repose,

And seems an Angel partly on the wing!
Life's pains are past, and agonies are o'er:—
But—stay! He yet revives and talks with God!
The peace of Heaven is Eden'd on his brow,
And smiles celestial play upon his lip;
From his bliss-brighten'd eyes of ecstacy
His full-plumed spirit looks out light of day
On bright pavilions of oped Paradise,
And shouts aloud these words with his last breath:

'God floodeth down a day of heavenly light!
His smiles play all around the sepulchre—
Immortal joys do blossom o'er the tomb!
Behind Death's door stands Immortality
With smile that days the grave with light of Heaven!
Celestial light divines the gates of Death,—
Lo! Death is but the messenger of Peace—
Could meet a thousand Deaths without one fear!
The Vale of Gloom, no darkness hath—no night,
And valley's end is throng'd with Seraphim!
All fills with God, and everything is Heaven—
The thought of Heaven is summer to the soul!
The Angels come! Archangels! Hierarchs!
My Savior comes with glory flam'd around—
The King of Glory in his beauty comes
To crown my brow with corona of stars!
My soul is gladness, for the Lord is near,—
The Passover is coming—Allelujah!
Wake—spirit! put thy crown of glory on;
Strike hands with those that wait to welcome thee,—

Awake! and wave thy palm of Victory:—
God says—'*To Father's bosom come, my son!*'
Is that sweet Heaven, I see? Yea—glory! glo—'

He told to Jesus what remain'd untold
When pass'd from labor to his great reward,
And left a smile upon his tranquil corpse,—
He smiled at Death, for God did smile on him.
His happy spirit pass'd from earthly things
As sweet as Beauty's bloom from cheek of flowers,
Or Zephyrus, from incense-breathing spring.
So near to God, he step'd from this world to
The next, without confusion, or alarm,—
So ripe for Heaven, his clay felt not Death's dart!
He conquer'd Death, not King of Terrors him—
Shouted Death-victor in the jaws of Death,
And died death-great—triumphant over Hell!
What floods of glory blaze from setting suns—
The golden Day's divinity expiring!
Thus, Christian died. My end be like to his.

O, IMMORTALITY! It dries the tear
That falls upon the urn of those we love,
And 'lumes with Glory's light the Vale of Death;
It smooths the deep death-steep, and lets us down
Softly to tomb, as downy feather's fall.
Oblivion's foe is Immortality—
Eternal triumph o'er oblivion!
The soul's life-time beyond the sleep of death,—
The god in man that makes man kin to God:

Death, is the stripping off this garment earth,
And all the rest is—Immortality.
His *mortal* slept, when his *immortal* woke
And flam'd away from Earth to be all Heaven:—
I can not think of him without heart-leaps
To strike glad-hands with him in Paradise.
O, Earth! thou hast lost much in losing him,
But cease my harp—Heaven hath an Angel more.

IN MEMORIAM.

In Memoriam.

ELEGY:

ON THE DEATH OF
MY SISTER'S MOST SWEET AND LOVELY LITTLE BABE,

RACHEL ANN JONES.

Born, October 15th, A. D. 1838. Died, August 23d, A. D. 1839. Aged 10 months and 8 days.

TO THE MOTHER.

Sister Julia:—You desired me to write a few lines on the Death of your sweet RACHEL ANN. This sheet contains them. But I fear, they sink far below your feelings on the subject. Ah! who can feel a Mother's Love, save her alone? Who mourn the Child in Death like her who bore it? None, my Julia—none. On her heart alone true Sorrow sits; and all her thoughts—the true sublime. Imagination, on her swiftest wing, can never reach a Mother's piteous moans, or sighs sublime, for her loved Babe in death; nor, at the fountain head of Sorrow, drain one tear, so pure, bright, beautiful as hers. Hope not, Sister, then, to find in all this Elegy, one thought worthy of your own. I wrote—wrote as I felt, and felt as I wrote. Then pardon, Julia, if I've wrote amiss, and let a Sister's love, smile out its heaven of charity on him

Who loves you with a Brother's love,

WOODMANSEE.

Elegy.

Is there on Earth one sullen soul
In Folly's school so harden'd grown,
That, in his heart—his blacken'd heart!
No sorrow finds to mourn the dead?
Not feel sweet Pity's soft control!
Nor drop the sympathetic tear!
That heart is *dead*—from mercy lock'd,
From light and life and joy and Heaven,—
All—all must weep, for—RACHEL'S DEAD—
That beauteous Babe with silver locks!
Mourn, O, my soul! and thou bless'd Harp,
My heart's delight in Sorrow's storm,
O, mourn! in doleful sorrow mourn
The Young and Beautiful in death!

Ah! Rachel Ann, thy hour how short—
How *very* short thy little hour!
How soon did Evening onward rush
To tread on Morning's sluggish heels—
Life-floweret nip'd e'er 'twas a-bloom!
Thou Eden-rose! thy form divine
Had too much Heaven to dwell on Earth
Where Sin so thickly sows her thorns
To hedge fair Virtue's narrow path
That leads to Happiness and Heaven.
All, all was done to stay thy flight,
And keep thee with us here below;

But *Aqua-vita* was as nought,—
Fell Death had thrown his cruel dart
Far, far beyond the Healing Art.

Thy little lamp of life went out,
But O, how bless'd! Heaven's lamp of Love
With rays divine did guide thee safe
Through valley of the shade of Death,
And Glory own'd one Seraph more!

To father fond and mother dear,
Thou wast the sweetest ray of hope—
The fairest, purest, brightest, best,
That ever smil'd with full of joy
On Life's rich coronet of love!—
Their may-day smile of happiness!
Their life's day-star of loveliness!
Their every rose-lip'd joy on Earth—
Soul-diamond and heart-jewel—thou!
Their Eden-blessedness and joy
That smil'd bright innocence as Heaven!
But smil'd not long—alas, for Life!
It came like lightning's speedy wing,
And then departed as it came!
'Twas over soon! that smile of Love
On perfect Beauty's lip a charm,
Was too divinely bright for Earth,
And *thou*,—celestial lily fair
From the empyrean bower of bliss,
On Earth thou bloomest but to fade,

Then, in the Garden fair of God
Flourish and bloom—eternally.

The fairest lily soonest fades,
And ripest beauty quickest dies;
The kindest, fondest, best beloved,
The soonest run Life's little race—
For Glory ripe e'er in their bloom!
Sweet Angel! thou did'st stoop to Earth
To weep o'er poor Mortality,—
On unbent pinion then return
To be the smile of Seraph's joy
And make bright Heaven more beautiful!
Bless'd Babe! when Gabriel's trump shall call
All Nations to Jehovah's throne,
How many Kings will wish their lives
Had been as short and good as thine!

Then, Mother! take thy last cold-kiss
And soul-relieving Fare-thee-well,—
This Mercy grants all merciful;
O, be content! she was thine own
When fair she smil'd upon thy knee,
Now she is Heaven's! with Angels smiles
As fair, as soft, as pure as Love
'Round her Almighty Father's throne:—
Each heart did bless her while on earth,
To bless her now—is Heaven's delight.

But lo! the mournful Mother weeps!
Ah! each bright tear, each groan and sigh

Doth sweetly echo in high Heaven—
'ADIEUS,' to her dear Rachel's shade!
For thee, sweet Babe! a heart-heaved sigh
From out my melting bosom comes,—
I weep—I weep, to see that face—
The smile of heaven, lie cold in death!
On my sad heart, soft Pity sits
With mournings like the dove,—
But nought avails—she will not wake
To bless her mourning Mother's arms!
Not streaming floods of Sorrow's soul
Can bring her back thro' all of pearl,—
Grief's shriek or scream of Agony,
Or thy deep-dismal wail—Despair!
The monster Death in cold embrace
Relentless holds his prisoner still!

O, cruel Death! why didst thou come,
And steal sweet Rachel Ann away?
Why nip the flower within its bud?
Why on the fair Defenseless prey?
Thou coward Death! on Infant blood
Slake not thy desperate thirst again!
Go heave the rocks from Andes' brow
And eat the flames from Etna's top,—
War with Whirlwind—with Lightning join
And Thunder close in dreadful fray:—
'Gainst these, thy bony arm employ,
But stain no more thy giant might
By laying the defenseless low.

How is Life fallen from her tower!
The Beautiful gone down to death—
Virtue a tenant of the tomb!
The Angels ever take their own.
Come, iron brow of scornful Pride,
And heart of adamantine Hate,—
In social sorrow lend one tear
To Infant Innocence in death.

HER EPITAPH.

From gentle sleep she woke
Life's cup to drain:—
'*Gall to the brim*,' it spoke,
'*And deadly pain!*'
From lily hand it fell,
She meekly sighed—'*Farewell,*
'*Life's cup is pain and hell,*—
I'll sleep again.'

Thoughts,

AT MY BROTHER'S FUNERAL.

O, weep not for the happy Christian dead!
Lament not that his day of mourning's fled;
Sin, dust, disease, no longer chain his soul,—
A *victor* over Death at Glory's goal!
Why should I weep my Brother's *liberty*,
His *triumph* over Death—his *victory?*
Death conquer'd, is his triumph, not his foe—
Gives worlds of pleasures for this one of wo.
Am I in tears because my Brother's free—
Free from all Earthly ills that compass me?
Do I lament that he laments no more?
That sore Affliction's living reign is o'er?
That all things are his own that soul can love—
Eternal-crown'd with Paradise above?
Doth his rejoicing ope my weeping eyes?
Why weep that Angels hail him in the skies?
Why weep that he hath gain'd Eternal-shore—
Eternal-lifed with pleasures evermore?
What, *weep!* that he is number'd with the Bless'd—
Retir'd from toil, and gone to endless rest,—
Hath chang'd his night-of-Earth for Heaven-of-day—
'T is all fell discord in a Seraph's lay!

O! why these tears of anguish and remorse
When Wisdom, Virtue cry—'*Rejoice—rejoice!*'

Let Grief and Anguish pour their floods of tears
O'er Sin and Folly's hope-forsaken biers;
Ay, Mourning Comfortless low-bend her o'er
Crime-living, or *Sin's-dead*, and ever pour
The gall of Spirit as her red eyes roll
Heart-agony death-mingled with the soul!
True Lamentation's groans aloud declare:
'Tears for the lost abandon'd to Despair;
Tear-showers of spirit rain from Sorrow's eye
O'er Hope's abandon'd—black Iniquity;
For living Crime, heart-tears of blood are due,
But—happy Christian! not one tear for you.'

Tears for a Saint, that his affliction's o'er!
Lament that Heaven hath gain'd an Angel more!
What! sunk to night of grief, that he is free,
Thrice happy in a bless'd Eternity!
Heart full of sorrow that his sorrow 's o'er!
Weep dolorous because he weeps no more!
Tears for the Saint! Lamenting comfortless
That he 's with God—rejoicing with the Bless'd!
Hah—TEARS! and not ecstatic joys of soul
That he hath gone where ceaseless raptures roll!
What—WEEP! that he 's from sin, death, hell, all-free—
Tear-drops on rose of Immortality!
What—MOURN! while Holy Writ—(Heaven's trumpet voice!)
Thunders for Christians all:—"REJOICE! REJOICE!"

The Crucifixion.

SUPPOSED TO BE WRITTEN BY AN EYE-WITNESS.

PART I.

When flaxen locks curled o'er my youthful brow,
And I sat playing with my infant joys,
My Mother caught me in her hasty arms
And mingled with a—Crowd!
                    Joy sat sublim'd
In every look, and Victory on each lip;
Ah, smiles! ah, joys! how soon to fade and die!
And dying—leave the sting of death behind!

'T is victory weak that mocks its foe's last groan;
'T is fiendish joy that laughs at dying sighs—
Infernal smile that smiles on Agony.
Accurs'd the *heart* that doth not sorrow feel
When soul bids clay farewell with parting pang;
Accurs'd the *hand* that would not turn aside
The dart of death from penitential tears;
Accurs'd the *eye* that fondly loves to see
The tooth of fell Disease in sunder gnaw

The soul and body of its enemy;
Accurs'd the God-defying wretch that mocks
While breaking heart strings fluttering **murmur** '*death!*'—
That monster curs'd, who loves, or joys to see
Fell Death astride the pillow of his foe
With pangs that break frail Nature utterly.

That Crowd's great joy was fiendishness like this!
Joy sat sublim'd and climax'd on her soul,
And smiles of triumph blossom'd on her cheek:—
That Crowd's heart-love was cruelty and blood,
The sweetest music to her dragon-ear,
And bath'd her soul in new delight and bliss!
The scene on which her eye long loved to dwell!
A field from which her hand reap'd richest fruits!
Garden replete with prospect beautiful
Of fruits and flowers of every kind and hue
That towering thought could think, or mind conceive,
And standard full of every luxury!

Ah, Crowd most damn'd, at war with God and man!
Ne'er look'd on Sorrow's sob, or Pity's tear!
Ne'er sigh'd with Sympathy! nor wept with Woe!
Ne'er smiled with Joy, or walk'd with Love to bliss,
Nor perch'd on flowery wing of Hope to soar
Above her home of perfect wretchedness!
But loved to feast where blood and slaughter roll'd
While death-pangs rent the cords that held in life,
And Carnage's hand enrichen'd all the plains!

PART II.

Now, busy Hate, with fiery eyes fierce stalk'd
And gave to Pride's high arm his thirsty spear,
Whiles foamy Wrath rose high and stir'd the fires
That fiercely burned in hot Revenge's breast;
And Vengeance dread whet sharp his desperate lance,
And gave it barb'd to fell Destruction's hand.
Hot cruelty shrieked out to Violence,
And look'd fierce daggers down on Mercy's brow:—
Defiance, Boasting, (as Heaven's thunderbolts
Aloud above the whirlwind's dreadful roar—
Death-horrors giving to the Elements!)
So they sped forth outrageous to destroy,
Defying Earth and Heaven—demoniacs!
Till Death—their woful captain! huge uprose
Apollyon-fierce—outraging Devils damn'd
And shook a dart of fury indignation-fired,
With earthquake-bellow, roaring—"CRUCIFY!"
All, firmly grasp'd their hot-avenging spears
And swords that sighed for blood, with demon-claws,
And swept forth tempests raging to devour,
Till Murder and Revenge just hot from Hell,
Nail'd JESUS to the cross of Agony,
And crucifi'd *Emanuel—God with us!*
Whose cross, became the only key, to ope
For Man, the pearly gates of Paradise.

And I—*was there!* among that horrid crowd!
O, woful thought! dark story of my life!
That hour be torn from Time's great calendar;

That time, from rolling years be blotted out;
That hateful scene, from Nature's book erased,—
O! be the day burn'd up in endless Hell!
That *Crowd*, sink in Oblivion's grave forgot!
Let awful Horror gnaw upon her there,
And desperate Woe forever howl her deeds!

Come—Pity! drop thy gall on Calvary,
For there the deed was done that shook the world—
O, wash that blood from her polluted top!
Mourn—O, my soul! in doleful sorrow mourn —
Ah! bleed afresh my heart! and ever bleed,
For woe is me—O, wretched and undone!
Flow out my tears—in quick succession flow
And drown mine eyes in deep, exhaustless streams,
For they, alas! they saw my Savior die!
Mine ears! forget to hear,—strike deaf, O, Death!
They heard Him groan:—'REDEMPTION IS COMPLETE!'
He hung aloft—the subject of all sport!
He bled upon a Cross twixt heaven and earth,—
The cross of Death by Murder planted firm—
Huge wooden cross from Aspen's silent grove,
But since renown'd for melancholy song.
He hung with Prayer, and bless'd His enemies!
Whose tongue was Truth, whose words redeeming love;
Whose actions grace, whose looks tranquillity;
Whose smiles were heaven, whose joy was bliss indeed;
Whose dying groans made dark the sun himself,
And bade great Nature weep in loud convulse.

He cried, 'I THIRST!" They gave him gall to drink;
'I THIRST FOR HEAVEN!' He groaned in agony;
Then, with that dragon-crowd, my Mother—laughed!
And I too—O, forgive me Jesus! *laughed*
Tho' little was my lip! He groan'd! the sun
In sorrow wept, and weeping hid his face;
But Man, with Devils grin'd, and mock'd and howl'd
Whiles Pain and Anguish rent his heart in twain!
Ah, with Revile reviled, with Scoff they scoff'd—
With Mockery and Eternal Mockery mock'd!
Sin's demon-claw, steep'd in Damnation's brink
Fell Envy, Scorn and Man, in friendship shook
With fiendish leer, and with such horrid grin
As show'd their snakish tongues and sulphur eyes
As flames of fire from their own native Hell.
He bow'd his head; Day tumbled from his throne
In deep and dead eclipse! whiles Midnight drear
On Darkness' ebon-wings vail'd earth as Hell,
And Peace and Quiet in their graves found Rest.

Now, deep Affliction sat upon His brow,
Whose deadly tusk gnaw'd greedily at heart,
Whiles Crucifixion's rod of anguish rent
Life's golden bands that soul to body bound,
Till faint Humanity with Wonder cried:—
"ELI! ELI! LAMA—SABACHTHANI?"
In loudest note! Then bowed His sacred head,
And bowing bade His spirit—God, farewell,
And Light of all things darken'd into death.
The hellish mob, with triumph howl'd aloud;

Hell heard, and shriek'd thro' caverns bottomless:—
I hear it still! That death-pang rent my heart.
I heard His death-cry and their mockeries,
And then I wept,—tears fell on Jesus' feet,—
My tears mix'd, mingled with my Savior's blood!
The blood that washeth every sin away.
'*Why weeps my child?*' surprised, my mother cried,
'*Nay, do not weep,—for shame! 'Tis only a*
Poor *Nazarene, call'd Jesus Christ the Lord!*'

Epitaphs.

ON METHUSELAH.

Nine hundred sixty-nine, I lived;
  Life was a breath, and pass'd :—
I did but grow and bloom and ripe
  To fade and fall at last.

EPITAPH.

When Death unlock'd Life's door to me,
I woke up—Immortality.

ON A CHRISTIAN.

Not 'neath the sod :—
Gone home to God.

ON A LITTLE GIRL.

The Innocent and Beautiful,
My Ida May the dutiful,
Turn'd Seraph at the age of Seven,—
"Of such, the Kingdom is of Heaven."

EPITAPH.

Retir'd from House of Clay,
And gone to—Endless Day.

ON A CHILD.

A child at rest,
By Jesus bless'd.

EPITAPH.

Life's dream is o'er—the spirit free,
And I am—Immortality.

ON A BABE.

O! happy Babe sleep on
From Sin and Sorrow free,—
In loving Savior's arms
Thy rest is heavenly.

EPITAPH.

A sinner I, redeemed by Grace,—
With Peace and Hope my ashes rest,
And I behold my Savior's face
In happy Mansions of the Blest.

ON MAN.

I'm all that tells Man ever lived;
I'm all that speaks—he 's not:—
Was born, and died, and buried here,
While all else are—forgot.

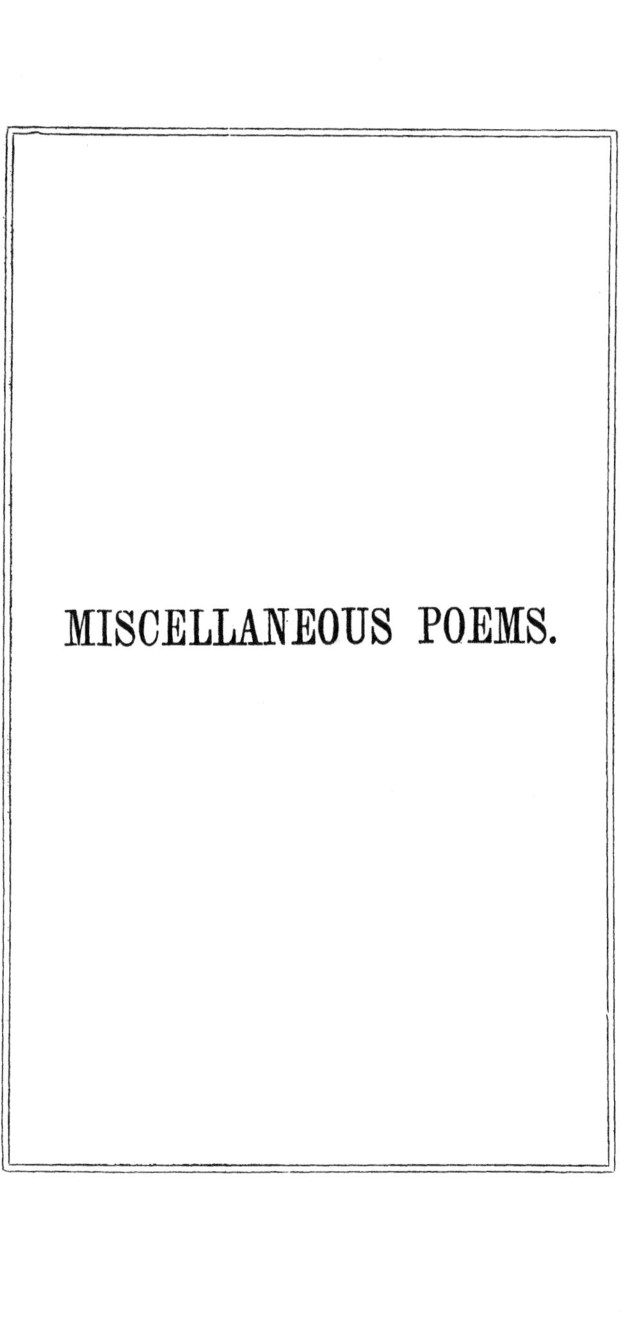

MISCELLANEOUS POEMS.

Poems of Childhood.

My Harp.

WRITTEN AT THIRTEEN YEARS OF AGE.

Awake my Harp! nor longer sleep when fair
Columbia calls—bright star of Liberty!
O! bind her brow with bright poëtic wreath,
Or shame Eternal haunt thee like a ghost
Whiles Time doth ride his years unto their graves,
And iron tongue with proclamation loud
Thunders to Earth my country's Epitaph:
"*Columbia had no Poet and she died.*"

HARP.

I'm yet too young! The ripening breath of Age
Hath not yet breath'd autumnal stores on me;
But when sublim'd with Nature's melody,
I'll wake to show proud England's boasting Muse
This truth indeed:—"*'Tis not Columbia's land
Where Genius sickens and where Fancy dies.*"

Childhood.

WRITTEN ALSO AT THIRTEEN.

O! I am now a jolly-romping boy,
In clean, white slips I dress all nice and coy;
And little tiny shoes all over red
Just for to on my mammy's carpet tread:—
O! how I do jump and how I do play
Till all the light hours fly fleeting away!
Then down on the hearth I tumble apace
And sweetly lay sleeping right jam on my face!
The cricket's chirping song close by my head,
Says plainly thus: "This child hath gone to bed."
My Mother sings: "Sleep on—sleep on my boy,
Thy father's hope, thy mother's constant joy."
Then, straight by gentle Dreams am I caress'd,
In all the fairy forms of Spirits dress'd.

Stormy Weather.

The flowers are dying—
Summer's loves!
The bright hours flying—
Cooing doves!
Now Nature pours her tears in showers,
Or crowns with snow the barren bowers;
The nightingale no longer sings,
No music thro' the woodlands rings;

All sweetest birds with merry jay
On painted pinions flee away,
And leave Man here to breast the storm,
Or build a fire to keep him warm,—
To warm his toes and shins together,
While fell without, raves—STORMY WEATHER.

Winter's Near.

Chill Winds are sighing
'*Winter's Near*,'.
While Autumn 's flying
With a tear!
And in the bird-forsaken bowers
Romp not the rosy-footed Hours;
The garden fades, the woodland moans,
And in her rock shrill Echo groans;
Faint whisperings run along the vales,
Low-breathing to the sickly dales:—
'Now, crown of glory falls from Autumn's head,
And Nature's loveliness lies withering—dead.'

Winter Weather.

The year was flying
With a groan,
And Zephyr sighing
With a moan,

When North-winds bellow'd out replying:—
'Frail Nature's loveliness is dying!
The valley's glow, the landscape's smiles
Are solitude in spirit wilds;
The owlet's hoot and jackal's yell
And panther's cry fill all the dell;
And snow and blow and frost and freeze,
Make bare the fields and strip the trees,
While cold and chill and storm together
Howl out to man of WINTER WEATHER.'

Winter Comes.

[A BOMBAST.]

Dread Winter comes—beware!
Beware the foe!
Or Nature's glory where?
Lain low—lain low.
He comes—he comes with power and might
The cheek of Loveliness to blight;
With storms and snows and frosts and rains
To bind our mother Earth in chains!
Fell Winter comes for war and fight
Creation's beauty all to blight!
Old Gray-beard comes! Let man beware!
To freeze our toes,—
Tyrant! compel—*our shoes to wear,*
And wipe our nose!

Winter's Here.

Autumn said dying,—
'Winter's near';
North came replying,—
'*Winter's Here!*
The Landscape's lovely smile to nip,
And blight the rose on Beauty's lip;
With frost and snow and wind and chill,
To freeze the river, run and rill,
To make the South, the frozen Pole,
Where howling Storms and Tempests roll—
OLD WINTER 'S HERE!'

Poems of a Later Date.

The Milk Maid.

When summer's sun had sunk to rest,
  And evening brown'd the dale,
A lovely, rose-complected miss,
  Came tripping o'er the vale;
Without a cap, or bonnet on—
  Her hair played with the gale,
And on a little half-bent arm
  Dangled her—milking pail.

Her white foot was the snowflake's fall,
  While on to barnyard speeding
With childish jollity and glee,
  For milk and for feeding:—
"*Hay, hay for old Muly,*" she said,
  And clumb the tall haystack,
When poor, hungry Muly ball'd out
  At lots and gobs i' the rack.

Now, pail in hand, the maiden said,
  "To milkin I will go,"
As three-legged stool adown she sat,
  And sung:—"So, Muly, so;

So, so, take supper now on hay,
  Then sleep till morning go,
And I'll awake thee at daylight—
  But, so! So, Muly—so!

So, Mule! You ugly thing you, so!
  Sich work I'll not endure,—
You switch your fly-brush in my eyes
  I'll lick thee jist so sure!
Then, so Mule—so! so now and ***hise,***
  You mean, old sow you, hise!
As on her stool adown she sat
  To milk her in a trice.

Two-handed miss with might and main
  Made fast the nectar flow,
Nor thought aloud of ought save this
  Queer song—"so, MULY, so!'
Though Muly stood still as a post,
  Her jolly song was—"So,"—
Loved ditty, dear to milk-maids all
  Her own—***so, Muly, so!***

But Muly now impatient grew—
  At nothing 't all I vow,
And little miss as hasty said,
  "The witches ails the cow!
Now Mule, you ugly huzzy, so—
  Why will you act up thus?
When every time I come to milk
  Thou kickest up a fuss.

You dirty, clumsy heifer you—
An old cow and so wild!
Hah! serpent of a critter you,
The witches have you spiled!
Now, so! you cross old varmint, so,—
You'd better so and hise!"
And rosy maiden's three-legged stool
Did give her beatings thrice.

"So, Muly—so,"—as miss's hand
Gave Muly's hip to "hise,"
"Now stand a little bit or more,
I'll milk thee in a trice:—
So, Muly—so,—so, slutty, so,—"
When lo! *stalk still she stood!*
That pretty maiden's pail was fill'd
While Muly—*chew'd her cud.*

To Robert Pollok.

See Scotia's Bard—"in humble dwelling born,"
To bless, refine and elevate mankind!
Bard of the heart and Poet of the soul,
Prince of the lyre and Muse of Holy Song,
Beloved on Earth but more beloved in Heaven,
Honor'd by men but honor'd more of God;
Religion's bless'd, fair Virtue's most approv'd—
Perfection's model and her brightest gem.
Bless'd Bard! by God's own hand thy harp was tun'd

On Time, on Life, on Death, Redeeming Love,
To charm with music sweet the Poet's ear
And feed with heavenly fruit the good-man's soul:—
Hail, holy Bard! by all the Muses bless'd
Poesy's chef-d'œuvre et ne plus ultra.

To John Calvin.

John Calvin, cease for Non Elect to pray,
Ah! canst thou turn black night to fairest day?
Their dreadful doom's inevitably seal'd,
And from their sulphur homes no power can shield.
John Calvin, cease for the *Elect* to pray,—
Well might the stupid ass to Luna bray;
Would'st surer make what God hath made most sure?
Or, purer cleanse Perfection's heart—most pure?
All mankind are *Elect* or *Non*, you say,—
Then tell me this, good John:—'*for whom you pray?*'
Thou canst not tell! Ho! then, sir, squalk out thus:
'*All prayer is vain and most superfluous!*'
Then, Calvin, why doth Holy Scripture say:—
'In everything give thanks and ceaseless pray?'

Mother and Babes.

A Mother smiles enchantment on her Babes!
Her bright, maternal smiles do brighten like
A day around the little, cherub-group,
Down-showering summer on the Eden-scene

Made sunny with affection of her heart.
Babes, round about, like rosy Cupids romp,
Her ornaments of admiration, love,
Her precious treasures beggaring Earth to buy—
The soft, the simple, tender little things!
Their plays, and artless prattle, wind around
The Mother's heart, demanding all her care
To train them up for Happiness and Heaven.
Full-feast and constant watch by night and day—
Sweet, spirit-mischiefs innocent as Loves!

Childhood.

In gentle Childhood's sunny hours
  No cares disturb'd my mind;
Of racking pains knew I of none
  Or sorrows could I find.

My heart was pure, my lips were clean,
  From sin and folly free;
I had not tasted of the fruit
  Of the Forbidden-tree.

I sat and talk'd the infant tongue
  In health and joy and glee;
And smiling sat like gentle May
  All on my Mother's knee.

Life's bud now opening to a flower
  Gave wilder joys to view;
And from that tender Mother's neck
  My little arms withdrew.

I sped to Sugar Valley's bower,
  Watch'd pretty Birds build nests,
Then sit upon the branches high
  And sweetly singing—rest.

And there, and then, my Harp awoke
  And its first sonnet sung,
Which oft in Manhood's riper hour
  With Angel-accents rung.

America.

America is but an *infant* yet,
Time's youngest born, but all a Jupiter
Arm'd with the lightnings and the thunderbolts!
And she shall yet cast off her cradle-clothes,
From swaddling-bands leap—*glory of the world*
With hand wide ope and heart benevolent,
And save her mother from a pauper's grave!
Smile-fac'd as Day, she looks to ends of Earth
With warm, heart-shaking hand to welcome all
Mankind, and crown their brows with—Liberty.

Hail, home of Equal-rights and Privileges—
Thou smiling Paradise of Plenty, hail!

Land of my birth, my manhood and my pride,
Where I have lived and loved and am beloved,
And Patriot-fathers sleep in christian-graves,
How art thou wed and oned with my fond heart!
But thy great name offends the Tyrant's ear,
And smites his soul with Envy and alarm
Ay, let him groan! thrones totter to a fall,
The morning breaks and light now days the world,
And he shall down, to gore Earth's heart no more,—
Crowns, thrones and scepters shall her footstool be,
For Man awakes to freedom—liberty.

The land where Genius is Archangel-winged
And Arts and Sciences are Wisdom-taught;
Where Liberty hath holiday the year
And Equity and Right with Mildness rule
In court of Justice and Equality:—
The land of Plenty and Prosperity
And Eden-bower of Piety and Peace
Where bless'd Religion looks unvail'd on God,
And Freedom smiles out heaven—imparadised!
America! the eye of all the Earth!
Lo! every clime hath found a home in thee—
All Seasons romp around thee all the year!
Thy mighty bound'ry is a hemisphere,
And measure of thy bosom—half a World!
Thy territory is a continent,
A proud immensity—world in thyself!
It takes the sun, in his celestial fields
Twelve hours, to day thee with the light of heaven:—

One half of Earth! where other half may fly
Oppression's scourge and Tyranny's and Want's,
And all mankind live as God made them—FREE,
And dare be men—the image of their God.

ON THE DECLARATION.

Her *Declaration*, is bless'd Freedom's chart
Baptised in Revolution's bloody sea,
And wrote with hearts of our heroic sires:—
'T is Liberty's own sword omnipotent,
And a death-thrust to Tyranny for aye,—
Columbia's boast and Earth's chief ornament.

Modesty.

Retiring *Modesty!* she'll walk one mile
Around, to keep from treading on a worm!
She is the handmaid of bless'd Innocence,
Demure and brightly beautiful as Truth—
All infant tenderness as soft as Love.
A shield of beauty is bless'd Modesty,
Her gentle brow has never learnt to frown,—
The first to listen, and the last to speak!
Blush-cheek'd she looks as heaven array'd in smiles,
Retires abash'd, her likeness to behold
In pictur'd mirror gazing on her charms,—
Abash'd the angel of her cheek to see—
Those star-bright eyes that look a living soul!
Then shrinks in self all tremblingly alone,
And vails herself—a blushing Modesty.

Gentle Love.

Soft is Love's hand, and silken too the chain
That kniteth hearts—to *one* heart mingles *twain!*
One honey moon is smiling all the year,
Nor winter's frown, nor scolding tempest near;
A meek, retiring gentleness is Love,
And innocent as summer-cooing dove;
As happy as bless'd Happiness can be—
Earth's joy that sips bliss of Eternity!
Affection, is Love's food; *neglect* he flies,
Lives in a smile, and by a frown he *dies.*
True lovers, are as gentle to their loves—
Gentle and tender as the cooing doves;
All infidels that 's found cold-hearted, sour,
Love's self expels from Hymen's rosy bower.

Soliloquy on the Gallows.

Now, joys of life—sports, loves, bliss—stand aside:
The Trap-door roareth out aloud—'*Make haste!*'
Groan on infernal Door, thy voice wakes soul.
My hope's despair, and thou my heaven's hell—
TRAP-DOOR! Death's door! Hell's gaping jaws on Earth,
Time's end—Grave's brink—road to Eternity!
Pit-fall of Crime—thou fleetest road to Wrath,
I'll on thee stand! Nay, sink fast from my feet,—

Bend, tremble, crack, break, fall, and let me to
Oblivion down, and feast eternal fires!
Then, Hell, groan on, and all ye Devils, howl!
Ye Damn'd—we meet! snatch me away, ye Fiends,
To your sulphurous home—infernal flames!
Fire-hills! we'll ride sublime profoundest Hell!

Lines.

Our rosy youth will soon be gone,
  Our Life itself shall fly;
Each passing minute weaves our shroud,
  And Time himself must die.

Departing hours now dig our grave,
  Past moments ope our tomb;
Day tumbles into night at eve,
  And reads to man:—'*Doom—doom.*'

But Virtue, smiles serene the while
  As on to Heaven she hies,—
Shouts o'er the grave and death and hell,
  'VICTORY!' while she dies.

Let Man—awake! seek Virtue *now*,
  Religion's call attend,—
Be "*born again*"—make Heaven thy home,
  And God himself thy friend.

Sarcasm.

His piercing features, stab, like poniard's thrust,
And make the blood stagnate all round the heart,
Or boil for vengeance while we gaze on them.
That cutting look shaves like a razor's edge—
Lightning in looks and thunder in his leer!
Heart-bane, wide purples on that lip of scorn
And shows it canker'd,—wormwood 's in his smile,
And every breath he breathes—bitter as gall.
His language cuts like clashing falchion's stroke,
And words, all bite,—there 's venom on his tongue!
A tongue as sharp as dagger's gleaming point—
Invenom'd tongue that poisons as it kills!
He hath the look that Satan's visage wears
Whiles crowing o'er a soul just damn'd, perchance.

Wonder.

What 's *Wonder?* Unrevealed Novelty
Unvailing self to eye of Ignorance.
The dam of Wonder is, white-eyed Surprise,
And his wretch'd father—soul-blind Nescience,—
No wonder he is neither horse nor jack!
With wild-bewildered eye and hair erect,
On Expectation's broad'ning wing—aghast,
Ahush he stands, all eye, all ear, all heart,—
A tongueless statue drinking in his breath!
He ever makes things greater than they are,

Gives form to objects Nature never framed,
Ay, life to Naughts that Fancy's self hath no
Conception of,—yea, magnifies to base
Monstrosities, Chimeras all invisible,
And peoples with more Anthropophagi
The vast grown heaven or hell of his surprise,
Than Night's wide spread concave can number stars!
At every whirl of his white-rolling orbs,
Old Chaos gives a new Creation birth.
To which, God's six-days'-work has nothing like,—
Monsters-of-monsters hideous and dire,
Such as ne'er denn'd in Misconception's womb,
Or, cloak'd them with Eternal shades—Hell-shadows!

Life.

On tall tree trembling
Sickly leaf!
Frail Man reminding
Life is brief.
Life's brightest path and sunniest hours
Are tangling wilds and fading flowers;
A Frailty on tomb reclining—
Both Life and Death in arms entwining.
Like flitting bubble in the stream,—
The painted romance of a Dream!
A meteor's glare, or flying feather,
One shoots, one bursts, and—gone forever!
A rainbow on the stormy spray,
Or moonbeam at the smile of day,—

How like the breath we blow on steel,
Or thrill of joy young lovers feel
While kissing bashful maidens meek,
Or, blushes burning on their cheek!
Or as the sunset's crimson light,
A moment more, and—*all is night!*

Silence.

On Silence' stilly lip there lives a soul;
Her look talks thoughts as loudly as a tongue—
The soul of Silence that speaks audibly!
She is the daughter of Eternity,
And born of Chaos and Nonentity.
She dwells in inward chambers of Repose,
And sits enthron'd with Quietude and Dreams;
She rests pavilion'd in the halls of Luz,
And sleeps in home of Secrecy and Death.

Dread Silence seems—pulse of Existence still'd,
A pause in Nature—breath of Being seal'd;
A death-profound in Time's wide solitude—
Lone Solitude upon the face of things!
Or, stamp of Breathlessness on lip of Life,—
A Life-stop quite beyond the vale of Dreams,
And tongue-rest voiceless as a sepulcher.
With noiseless foot, on back of Calm she treads—
Mum Quiet holding back the winged Winds!
Or, floats on bosom of Vacuity

As soft as spirits glide on midnight wings,
Nor dreams that Sound hath ever voic'd its name
In vast Creation's ever listful ear.
She, tongueless stands, nor dares to think aloud,
A breathless statue and a speechless shade,—
A fearful Stillness villainously still—
Chain'd-soul, dumb-mouth'd, yet promising to speak!

The Painter.

His rainbow-pencil was celestial-hued,
And flesh and blood grew 'neath his magic-touch.
His canvas, started into life, and look'd
Creation, glowing with the smile of God!
His Pictures mirror'd Nature's every Grace,—
Ay, there young Beauty rose with snow-bank breast,
And summer-cheek where living roses play'd,—
Where spirit-talking eyes, words-speaking mouth
And lips bloom'd into life, and smil'd out—*soul!*

Flattery.

Lip-good and hollow-hearted Flattery
Feeds all her victims with an empty spoon,
And thro' a bubble and a vapor-breath,
She oft robs Samson's brow of manly locks
Till Greatness' self is weak as other men—
Smooth-tongu'd hypocrisy, oil'd to deceive!

Ay, a sly-creeping, baneful viper she
Hid in rose-bower to ruin and destroy:
A seeming Friendship licking Vanity
From head to foot to swallow her alive
Without the slightest danger to herself!
She is a counterfeit Hypocrisy
That pays off Vanity as with good coin.
She hath a charmer's tongue and viper's heart;
Her serpent-tongue is double—falsehood all
Gloss'd with deceit and honey'd o'er with lies,
And guiles and charms of Mischief are her smiles;
Her words are varnish'd over by Deceit,—
Her speech deceives, and promises betray.
She oft bows low with hollow-hearted look,
And cloaks with white rob'd Truth, her blackest lies;
Ay, Flattery's words all polish'd scabbards are
In which fell Ruin's daggers are conceal'd.

To Mary.

WRITTEN IN HER ALBUM.

A century hence, dear girl, and where
  Will this loved Album be?
This small memento of respect,
  And Mary—thou? and—me?
A *Century!* who shall see that day
  As once they did of old,
That came and pass'd and it was not
  Like story that is told?

An hundred years! how long it seems,
And yet how quickly fled!
But fewer *days* than *months*, perhaps,
We're number'd with the—*dead!*
Then let us up, and all alive
To Wisdom's wisest rules,
That Demons may not call us 'theirs,'
Nor Death:—'*Time's silly fools.*'

Ah! sleep not now—be all awake,
Our life exists by flying;
Of but one moment, Time is made—
That moment is a-dying!
O! let us on thro' Virtue's paths
To bless'd Religion wed,
And number'd be among the saints
When number'd with the dead.

Contentment.

Behold *Contentment!* calm reposing on
The happiness of her own heavenly thoughts,
While soul flows out to God—all adoration
For peace of mind, contented Poverty!
Contentment 's rich, in knowing not her wants;
She is Life's wealth, and Wisdom's blest estate,
And she can make the poor man's little, great,—
So sanctify the crum of Poverty
That board of Luxury, compar'd, is want,

And wealth of kings, a gilded wretchedness,—
A servant bearing every burden—she!
Her life, is one long christmas holiday;—
On acorns can she find a royal feast,
And from the crystal brook, pure nectar sip.
She bares her bosom to Misfortune's dart,
Stands face to face with fell Adversity,
And looks unshaken on Calamity:
Her eye can gaze on Heaven, and her calm soul
Have no desire, or wish to speed—homeward!

Patience.

World-moving and God-wrestling Patience sits
With Happiness, Peace, Safety and Content
In Eden-bower of bless'd Tranquillity
And hath a heaven to go to Heaven in!
Her arm is short, foot slow, and dumb of tongue,
But, loss of empires unto her are dust,
The diamond coronets of kings, but trash—
World-riches dross, and all Earth-glories vain.
Her bark of faith is anchor'd to its God—
A living hope without a doubt or fear,
And built upon by Immortality.
Her soul superior to Misfortune's storms,
She triumphs over Difficulty's self—
Unmoved by thunders of Adversity.
She knows of truth, Life hath no Hadean-depth
To which her kind Protector can not reach,

And bring her up to light and life again,
And crown her with Prosperity and Heaven.

The Mother.

She is Man's happiness and his life's crown,—
God's six-days' labor was complete in Eve.
Around a Mother, joys, affections, loves
Revolve, as stars around a central sun.
Her children, live in light of her sweet smiles
And laugh to flowers while meeting her caress,—
The Empress of a little world of Babes!
She wreaths to curls their soft and careless hair,
Plays with their tiny fingers with delight,
Then rocks their spirits into fairy dreams
On soft, maternal breasts that swell full-orb'd—
The nectar-founts from which they drink out life!
On bosom's softness cradled and asleep
To dream of peace, love, happiness and Heaven!

Mother and Babe.

Her happy looks speak out aloud to all:—
'*I jostle all the world upon my knee!*"
Both Joy and Hope are sunbeams in her eyes
Whiles on her lap with smile of innocence
Her heart-joy sleeps with look as bright as flowers,—
Rose, lily-cheek'd, where Health and Beauty glow

With light and life out twinkling all the stars!
Her world of care soft-cradled in her arms—
Young Innocence and infant Loveliness
To peaceful slumber lull'd and dreams of Heaven
By Mother's heart love-beating for her Babe!
A love-joy and a feast by day and night—
Love's own fair semblance in the human form,
And Jacob's ladder to its Mother's heart!

Perseverance

Bless'd Perseverance prospers evermore;
He doth remove each stumbling-block from path–
To every barrier the wreck and grave!
Ay, scythe-like Perseverance mows down all,
And wedge-like cleaves the knotty oak in twain.
His moveless spirit 's fixt as throne of Doom,—
His soul unshaken anchor'd to its God.
Strong Perseverance works with God-like power,—
His mighty arm 's almost omnipotent,
And his Life-wrestle is—*as with the Fates.*
His mountain-path, onward to Glory leads;
Now, Difficulty's Hill he climbs to top,—
Fame's temple storms, and—*takes it by his might!*
He 's one whom iron-arm'd Adversity
Can not subvert, or Danger's self subdue:—
Right onward goes until Resistance's self
Grows weary of the strife, and yields him—Heaven.

Life's Journey.

Now, orient Morn threw wide the gate of Day,
To smile on Earth with rosy-footed May;
Rose-tinctur'd Light sip'd nectar from the flowers,
Whiles lovers young sat smiling in their bowers;
Sweet Nature glow'd the loveliness of day—
Awoke from couch of sleep the wise to pray.
No sick'ning vapors, fogs, or clouds above—
Creation breath'd of melody and love!
But soon, a deadly mist, and gloom came o'er,
And blackness, with the angry thunder's roar:—
Tremendous night to follow morn so sweet!
How oft LIFE'S JOURNEY smiles—smiles thus to cheat!
It hath its sunny Morn, its glorious Noon,
Black Night—all fickle as the waning Moon.

When all the ambient air breathes favoring gales,
The fleetly flying ship in safety sails;
But when dread surges leap, and oceans roar,
And tempest thunders and the torrents pour,
O! how the frail ship cracks! How wild she's toss'd
Drove onward by Despair to Ruin—lost!
'T is likewise thus on Time's tumultuous sea,
When *Life*, like a pert bubble glides with glee,
While Breezes romp and gentle Zephyrs play
And gives to Mortals one short holiday!
But, when storm-clouds of sore Affliction roll,
And Trouble's thunders smite to prove the soul—
Alas! soon poor Mortality shall fall
To dust—all dust, and shrouded by a pall!

Washington.

The first in wisdom, and the first in might,
Crown'd one of Peace, and the strong arm of fight:—
The live-long day he braved the cannon's roar,
While all his armor stream'd with human gore;
From his resounding shield and clashing sword,
The mighty din of dreadful battle roar'd;
His hero-leveling sword met armor flashing,
As death-stroke following death-stroke fell crashing,
And gave to Liberty's invading foes
As many bloody graves as deadly blows.
Our gurdian, he, the States around confess'd,
And his paternal care, whole nations bless'd.
His death, pall'd Hope, and made a world his bier,
Freedom a grave, and Liberty a tear.

Honor.

God's nobleman, and greater than a King!
On brow, sits spotless Reputation's crown
Of priceless worth beyond a monarch's own,—
He frowns contempt down on all littleness.
His tongue is truth, and knows not how to lie,—
Speaks what he thinks, and thinks whate'er he speaks,—
Deceit and guile are not upon his lips.
His noble mind conceives no evil thoughts,
And heart, approves of nothing but the right—
The soul of Honor anchor'd to its God!

High Honor, image of bright Virtue is,
And shines sun-like—his glories blazing round,
Whiles Envy, in his presence stands appall'd,
And hangs her head condemn'd—tongueless and dumb!
No tongue can speak his name, or sum his worth
And not be Eloquence itself and Praise.

Dishonor.

Dishonor is—death-blight on character,
A Time-dug grave, down-swallowing alive,—
Good-name with wounds of Degradation dying.
He 's little in great things, and mean in little,—
His meddling fingers all require a watch!
His crimes, have paled his cheek, and snak'd his eye
Till his hang-head-guilt-look speaks—'*Villainy:*'
A Cain-mark'd wretch that hangman's rope shall hang!
So lost to Virtue and all nobleness
That he hath now, no honor to preserve,—
To Infamy flies, down long paths of Shame!
Tho' every step be crime, he onward sweeps
By Folly led, and Degradation hurl'd
With ruin down to Pandemonium.

Truth.

Truth, is, the speech of all the sainted ones,
The voice of Justice, Equity and Right—
Soul-purity drop'd from an Angel's tongue!
The tongue and language of the Heaven of Heavens,

And God himself is the *Eternal Truth.*
Truth's potency dispels the mists of Doubt—
Sincerity unvail'd to eye of day!
Its light, drives Error from the minds of men
And hurls Deceit and Falsehood down to Hell—
A potent sword to fight the Devil with!
Where Trnth is not, Apollyon hath his home.

Falsehood.

She hath Hell's look—is a Beelzebub!
The father of all Lies is her dread sire;
She leap'd from his sin-brain—all legion-tongued!
Her dragon shoulders grow three Gorgon heads
All devil-featur'd, and they look out—Deaths:
From her Crime-brazen brows of impudence
Fire-eyes glare wild—malignity of fiends,—
Fiend-grins on lips and Satan in her heart!
Her breath, infects the atmosphere round Earth,
And Upas-like spreads desolation out.
She roars out libels on the name of God,
And drives man to insanity and Hell:—
She is Hell-born, a Hydra fang'd and claw'd,
Death of Religion and the life of Vice.

Spring.

Now, bride-like Spring adorn'd with flowers
Walks forth with Love to wed the Bowers;
Her birds, give solitude a voice,
And speaking woodlands all rejoice;

Young Zephyr shakes from music-wing
Her balmy odors on the spring;
To Breeze's whistle day and night
Loved Flora frolics with delight,—
Her rosy smile gives birth to flowers,
And fruit and fragrance to the bowers.
Birth-day of Beauty, Song and Cheer—
Millennial glory of the year!
Where Health and Loveliness e'er meet
To bid the Edened Earth—'BE SWEET!'

The Tongue.

"The tongue is a world of iniquity."—HOLY WRIT.

Can any mythographer spy out,
With his owl-eyes that roll through heart of night,
And guess this myth: *What is the* TONGUE *of man?*
This Gordian knot of God's own handiwork—
Phenomenon in creation's mighty book,—
The wondrous wonder of this mystery solve,
And ope the riddle to the light of day?
'T is dark as embryo in Chaos' womb:
I'll speak to *Tongue*, mayhap she'll blab it out.

Thou dark enigma, never understood,
Though gabbling ever on in endless rounds,
Tom Thumb 's thy stature, strength, Goliath's might!
O'er Falsehood's purgatorial world of lies
Thou reign'st a very Satan in thy way,

O'erruling Adam's race, and proudly eminent,—
Earth-wooing siren charming to devour!
Thou judgment-blinding, will-perverting imp,
Soul-winning, heart-defiling wickedness,
How eloquent thy gab when all 's deceit!
But blind, stiff, lame and halt, thou stumblest on
O'er Truth's strong tale of facts, and ever hobbling!
O, root of evil! Varnisher of lies!
Firebrand of Envy—Falsehood's battle-ax,
Why lying ever *down* as invalid
To tell thy lies till Doomsday calls for thee?
Behold! the body's members, save thyself,
(Thou mouth-jail'd criminal!) are all *erect!*
Art sore diseased, or wearied nigh to death
With running 'yond the antelope in might!
If so, why flying still as foot of Health?
If sick, 't is not for want of exercise,
For I am witness to thy ceaseless gab.
Disease should give to feebleness repose.
Thou art the race-horse of Iniquity,
Whereon Hell's legion host of Lies let loose,
Chase through that Satan-seat—the human heart
And bring God's wrath upon the sons of men.

Deceit, in Falsehood's endless web of lies,
Thou art unbridled, though God bridled thee!
Art coffin-shaped, and rooted to thy grave—
The grave God dug for thee in jaws of man!
'T is well thou art confined by triple wall,
Of flesh, enameled bone and crashing jaws;

Thy liberty would be creation's blot—
Babel-confusion and earth's bedlam, thou!
Small lump of dirt, but a huge misery!
Pollution-bundle "set on fire of hell!"
Iniquity's own poking-stick red hot!
Of all ungovernables the most ungoverned—
Of every monster the most monstrous, base,
And yet, of all we love, the best beloved!
Man's greatest friend, his worst of enemies,—
Man's play-doll, that oft bruises his own pate!
The joy of soul, the hate of every heart—
True beauty, grafted on Deformity!

When our heart-dial is by Virtue set,
Then will the Tongue—that pendulum of soul,
Count truth o'er by the hour—*wag on aright!*
Woe's own elixir and the joy of Grief!
Full noon to Melancholy's cloudy day—
An every-day balm to Life's lonely heart!
An Aqua Vita for the ills of Time!
Full fount of happiness to Adam's race,
And Friendship's presence with the sons of men,—
Love-wand uniting heart of human kind!

Thou ready porter at the door of speech—
Exhibitor of heart, soul, mind and man—
Whole band of music to the World's great ear,
Thou art as gassy as an air balloon!
Wildfire, that sets whole neigborhoods by ears—
The fire that touches off earth's battle-gun,

To spread Destruction out from pole to pole,
And widen Desolation's path to hell!
The greatest evil, and the greatest good,—
Of good, the *better*, and of bad, the *worst!*
If wrong thou wag'st, Iniquity 's thy name;
If right, the greatest blessing to mankind.

Can Webster's great nomenclature speak out
Ten-million-tongued in its omnipotence,
And with Truth's wand portray to mental eye
That contradiction called "*the human Tongue*,"
So that the renegade where'er she strays,
May be brought back according to the laws,
And to her prison-cell confined for aye?
Words can't describe the indescribable,
Nor language speak what 's inexpressible:—
Phenomenon and myth! 'bove all that 's dark,
Enigma darkest, I leave thee i' the dark!
For, could my Orphic lyre sing endless rounds,
It ne'er could sing thee well as thine own—BLAB!

Humility.

Have mankind aught of which they should be proud?
Have they one thing that truly is their own?
Their very dust, the grave proclaims, "*is mine.*"
While man 's a tenant on his Father's smile,
Stayer in life-leased hovel of the dust,
His proper place and most becoming robe

Is deep HUMILITY—the only garb
That can hide poverty so squalid, vile,
The only dress God gives and angels wear—
Purest on earth, and brightest in the skies:
Man should be humble with his earthly lot
When all he hath, or can have is but dust.
Sure, pride and folly were not made for man;
They dug hell's pit and clothe a Lucifer,
But, fit man's back as a vast giant's robe
Loose-dangling on a Lilliputian.
True Greatness is forever meek and wise,
As Folly is both arrogant and proud;
Devoid of grace and sense, how hard is it
For a poor worm to be still a poor worm,
When nursed upon the lap of luxury,
And fann'd by wing of bright prosperity!
Wine of Prosperity makes giddy fools;
For man 's a very frailty itself—
A feebleness on-tottering for a fall,
And plung'd will be to Pandemonium,
'Less stretch'd-out hand, strong to deliver, saves.

Vale of humility 's at Jesus' feet—
The valley low of humbleness and love,
And peaceful vale of holiness and heaven
By stiff-neck'd Pride rejected and despised!
That deep-sunk vale of Christian blessedness
Deep down to dust of self-abasement sunk,
Where soul hath all her goings out to God—
A soul-prostration groaning up from dust!

Here we may empty self out of proud self—
Come out of self, and true salvation find,—
To nothing sink, and find ourselves with God!
Self, emptied of itself, grows full of God,
And humbleness is heaven'd at Jesus' feet.
If we lay here, the Lord will take us up—
Humility and meekness God exalts;
When in this vale of Christian holiness
Contrition prays, God hears him in high heaven,—
He stoops to hear Humility's deep groan,
And hearing grants—forgiving every sin.
Man's place is dust of deep Humility;
It is Mortality's defense through life,
Her tower of strength against a world of foes;
It is a shield 'gainst earth and hell combin'd;
Sackcloth and ashes move the throne of God,
And save great Nineveh from Sodom's fate!
Not Satan's power can harm Humility,
Or her white robe of innocence defile.

Look at God's Son, and see humility—
Cloth'd with humility as with a robe!
Christ was in stable born. Should I wish more?
A God-like virtue is Humility—
Humility's deep vale of holiness
By stiff-neck'd Pride rejected and despis'd,—
I almost worship thee—simplicity!
God is in love with this celestial grace,—
His chosen ones as little children are;
They 'd be earth's scoff to be salvation's heirs;

Mean in men's eyes, but greatness in their God's;
The poor in spirit he hath chosen his.
The meek and humble man alone is great;
He lives above the things of time and sense,
Converses face to face, and walks with God,—
The man that Heaven delights to honor—he.
Man's highest throne is at his Savior's feet,
And only way to Heaven is on his knees.

Psalm of Life.

On Time's life-wrecking sea we ride—
Secure from every ill!
God bids each threat'ning billow rise,
Speaks, and the storm is still.

Tho' sickness, sorrow, pain and death,
Disturb our pillow'd rest,
They can not rob soul of its heaven,
With God's own presence bless'd.

The sun may stay his car of fire,
And day at midnight wake;
But God will not forget his bride—
His own elect forsake.

Then trust in Him, ye faithful few,
And let vain doubtings cease,—
His pleasure works thy endless rest,
And presence-felt, thy peace.

Help me, O, Lord! in thee to trust,
  And on thy grace depend,—
My portion be and sure defense,
  My teacher, guide, and friend.

Make me a temple of my God,—
  Wed me to Virtue's ways;
Be all my thoughts God-worshipers,
  And every breath—thy praise.

Soul's Worth.

Omnipotence spake Being into life,
But Trinity in council—made the *soul*,—
That ornament of Heaven—light of the world
And God in man, a Savior died to save!
'T would bankrupt earth, to pay the price thereof;
'T would undo man to barter it away,—
Man's greatest wisdom is his soul to save,
For soul shall live when Heaven shall be no more!
A Babylon in wreck 's far less a wreck
Than the eternal wreck of one poor soul—
Of priceless price beyond the tongue to tell.
Bright Eve, with all her radiant wealth of worlds
Is not so glorious to All-seeing Eye
As *Soul* with Heaven's bright gem Religion in 't.
Weigh worlds,—Night with her coronet of stars,—
Weigh Being with all Heaven in her arms,
Then weigh the *soul*, and it outweighs them all!
Worlds shall grow old, and back to nothing turn;

The twinkling stars dim-eyed shall pass away,—
The heavens and earth all into atoms riven,
But *soul* shall laugh Destruction's frown to scorn,
And o'er the ocean-flame of burning death,
Trim its immortal pinions forth to God,
And live with Him, when Death himself is dead,—
The all that is immortal this side Heaven.
Canst tell the worth of the immortal soul?
It silenced Heaven half hour to answer it,
And answer came when Jesus gave himself!
Soul to redeem, the Lord of Glory died—
The Savior died to save the soul from death!
'T is precious, then, as precious blood of Christ,—
It made Heaven poor to buy it back to life.
Image of God, redeemed by God's beloved!
Sum up the worth of every drop of blood
The Savior shed, and that we'll call *soul's cost,*
And paid by Him who only knows its worth.
Then let the bright Immortal be our all;
Throw earth away, but treasure soul with care—
Gem sacred, and beyond all price as Heaven!
Bright in Salvation's wardrobe let it shine
In armor of Eternal Righteousness.

The Tyrant.

A *Tyrant*, is the chosen scourge of man;
A head, who rules all others but himself,—
Crown'd thief, that plunders groaning nations round
Of life, of all—according to the law!

One whom all fear, and no man ever loved,—
The Tyrant—fiend! another name for—Devil.

He sits upon his scull-based throne supreme,
Steep'd with perfume and glittering in his gold,
And makes realm poor, to make him demigod!
Looks empire round, and governs with a nod,—
The nod that robs his slaves of happiness,
And binds on back of wretched servants all
Life-crushing burdens—merciless as Death.
He speaks! His servile people all obey,
And Nation's peace hang on his breath—a mote.
His breath is law; his words are statute-books,—
Both life and death are trembling on his voice!
On distant countries writes:—"*Rex Omnium*"
With blood of kings by him annihilated:
O'er fellows reigns with scepter arm'd with might,
Till slavery's chains are round a kingdom's heart,
And kind death comes relieving from all wo,
Makes all the people slaves,—then robs and slays,—
A basilisk that strikes his thousands dead.

When blindness and injustice grasp the sword
Of Pow'r—Right, Justice, gasp, and live no more;
Imperial Power's a fearful thing in hand
Of error-blinded and sin-govern'd man;
How oft have low-born Immorality
And cloven-footed satan Tyranny
Sat throne of kings, and scepters sway'd to scourge
The world, and buy the hatred of mankind!

The one-man Power unmakes all other men:—
A golden *scepter* and a diamond *crown*,
Can make what Nature hath made *little*—GREAT!
Yea, cause the base-born blood of plebeian
To metamorphose into *Royalty*,
And so divine the veins wherein it flows
That *hinds* turn—*Tyrants, Emperors and Kings!*

Earth should build dungeons for them, but not thrones,
Or give to swords, 'stead scepters grant to them;
Then Liberty would rise and smile on Peace,
To find that man is as God made him—*free.*
It would be well with Tyrants, likewise Earth,—
They would not then to lawless *monsters* turn
And make wretched Earth the victim they devour.

The Old Black Ram.

A FABLE.

A weary Gardener threw away his spade,
Re-wip'd his sweaty brow, and sighing said:—
"A gardener's life 's made up of toils—troubles,—
Shall I sweat life away to gain bubbles?
I'll leave to base-born Toil and dust-wed swains,
To reap these nothings and to store the gains."
He ceased, and left his Eden situation
To find some happier occupation.

For twelve long months he traveled land and sea,
But business found he none from labor free:

For fortune long he sigh'd, for wisdom sought,
But found them hedged by diligence and thought.
He compass'd earth awide from shore to shore,
Professions, many tried—ay, by the score,
To sigh this truth aloud:—"Rich, wise, I see
Through life have been as busy as the bee;
And they that store their dust with greatest pains,
Reap most of toil and trouble for their gains.
Alas! have I now sought the wide earth o'er
My error but to find, and to deplore?
Then, back to native land—to garden flee—
Dear home of peace—sweet land of Liberty!"

When half way home his journey he had made,
By chance he spied a Shepherd in a shade,
Lolling at ease an idle hour away,
Where merry breezes romp, and zephyrs play:
The gardener said,—"A Shepherd's life is glee,
From toil and danger and affliction free,
No cares at heart, no troubles haunt his mind,
His Eden-home might make life half divine!
He lolls shade-couch'd, while tuneful pipe doth keep
Bucolic-strung, twelve-acres-filling sheep!

"My good, sir, Shepherd,"—now our gardener said,
While he approach'd the man and scratch'd his head;
"Are you not free from all the toil and strife
That midnight earth and thorn the path of life?
You're gay as lark, and merry as the jay,—
A shepherd's life is Idleness at play!"

"Nay, nay," the shepherd said, "I tell thee—nay,
Toils, cares, are round about me night and day;
Storms, tempests, blights, and other woes of earth
Are frequent interrupters of my mirth;
There 's bloody wars 'twixt savage beasts and I,
And oft I know not which of us shall die;
Sometimes a score of sheep do stray away,
Like erring men from virtue's heavenly way.
Though now the flocks seem innocent and gay,
Yet bloody wars they have as well as play;
Behold, yon Old Black Ram with horned head,
A score of rivals he hath smitten dead!
Bell-weathers all, whose heads are battle-proof,
Do fall before him, or must stand aloof:—
Old Thunder-head is up! and nigger-like as Ham—
Look! mercy, man! take care—*The Old Black Ram!*"

With bruises many and with bloody nose,
And much ado, the woful Gardener rose;
He leaped the hedge and eyed the ram despised,
Whilst to himself he thus soliloquized:

MORAL.

"Sure, gold is nowhere found without alloy;
Griefs, troubles, vail the sunny face of Joy;
E'en honey-bees have stings—each rose its thorn,
And down to death, life tumbles all forlorn;—
Ah, Earth! though thou seem'st guileless as the lamb,
I find in all thy ways—THE OLD BLACK RAM!"

Learning.

Sage Learning is the eye of mind wide ope,
The life of Understanding that days soul,
And sun that lights up Wisdom's orient noon;
The food, growth and expansion of ourselves,—
One long, lone life-inquiry after God.
She blazes day to heaven the world with light,
And bid god Knowledge king the throne of Mind;
Wisdom and Honor lean upon her arm,
And Science hath his life and light from her;
Aye, star-eyed Learning is handmaid of Heaven,
With bright Millènnial glory in her smile!
Where she is not, Egyptian darkness lowers,—
Her banishment is Chaos come again.
She ever brings great out of little things,
And her sons grow up giants all around!
She is the light, life, glory of the world,
And she like Virtue, is her own reward.

Wit.

Wit is the lightning of the mind, the true
Sublime of fools, or—Wisdom out of wits!
True Genius lodged in huge deformity;
Eyes wink, and grin of every lip around
Wit sits upon the throne of Jollity,
And doth electrify the soul of Mirth
While convuls'd Laughter holds his splitting sides.

Wisdom.

Sage Wisdom, is in part, the gift of God,
But Application seems his earthly sire,
And his loved mother patient Study is—
Those foes of Error and old Ignorance.
His towering forehead picturing intellect,
Speaks ocean-depth of thought dwells in his mind,
And from his eyes the spirit's lightnings leap
Alive, and glow God-light—immortal soul!
His eyes of fire, soul flashing, wisdom look,
And see unblinded to the heart of Night.
On his broad brow, sits Meditation deep—
Intensity of thought that days the world
And gives to man inventions new and strange;
Each feature talks of intellectual strength;
His looks announce:—God's image wrought in clay,
A God-made man, and molded from the dust—
From self-same earth that Adam was composed,
And passers-by exclaim—"Behold a Man!"

His home's seclusion and lone solitude,
Where soul awakes and Mind unearths itself—
Re-born, and ripened by far-reaching thought,
Out speaking loud to all Posterity,
And wisdom-filled, as hand fills up a glove.
He oft unnoticed stands, lost 'mong the crowd,
And seems if Heaven's in converse with his soul—
Mind full of vast conceptions all profound!
Modest, reserved—speaks little and says much,

For he e'er loves to think, while Folly talks
To show her lack of all things but a tongue—
An all-tongued nothing and iniquity!
Reflection is his spirit's mighty wing,
And Truth proclaims: "My seal is on his lips."

Deep, patient thought, sits crown'd upon his brow—
Crown'd like a king with Science's sacred stores!
In full meridian of his wisdom's blaze
He reigns on throne of Greatness—Honor-crown'd,
And ever hath his foot on Folly's head.
Sage Reason, on his mind exalted sits;
His eye looks thro' the mists of Ignorance
Where all is night to Mediocrity,
And sends mind forth to rove the regions vast
Of Error, Doubt and Gloom, till Certainty
Leaps forth from Darkness and Uncertainty;—
He grasps old Mystery and makes her his,
And with Investigation moves the world.

To all the starry hights of wisdom towers!
All gems of learning sparkle in his mind,
And wealth of knowledge fills him with her stores;
From the deep well of science draws—world-light!
His soul of light unmasks blind Nescience
And unto human vision opes noon-day,—
Reads starry skies familiar as a book,
And takes great Being captive at a thought.

A mid-day sun that lights Posterity,—
A sun to light the age in which he lives—

The light of Mind as day of universe
And constellation to Futurity!
His eagle eye looks vast creation through—
He looks thro' Time and Life's dark mist of years
And holds communion with Eternity.
He talks with death familiar as a friend,
And dreads the grave as little as his bed;
He wears his earth about him as his robe
Loosely, that he may drop it in the grave
Without regret, as soon as Death's bell rings,
And speed to many-mansion'd Heaven—all God's!
His life-deeds can not know oblivion,
They shine—the guide for ages yet to come,—
Born to be Wisdom to posterity!

Genius.

The history of true Genius is Woe's own,
And written too by Tribulation's hand:
A foundling she, in Poverty's low vale,—
In some by-corner, up from ashes springs
A bright Divinity, that Common-place
E'ermore condemns to gibbet, jail or rack,
And howls aloud: 'Let her be crucified!'
Lives while she lives on crumbs, and dies in rags;
But, Phenix-like, her ashes do revive
And wake to live an Immortality—
The praise and glory of Posterity.

She is an Angel fallen from her Heaven,
Therefore a stranger to this mundane sphere;
And Earth, is too owl-eyed to see the god
That came to life the Mind with living light
And day soul's deep-down cell with heavenly fires;
The laugh and scoff, one of the other is,
E'er at antipodes as pole to pole.
Let Genius stem the world's loud laugh and scoff
As eagle's wing the hurricanes of time,
And hope for smiles and a clear sky beyond,
And thither ply her planet-sweeping wing.

She is original, thinks for herself—
Originality deep as a sea!
Invention, is her fort and her strong tower,—
Discovers all things that's discoverable,
And is creative like Omnipotence,
Whiles Wisdom, parrot-like, *learns* all he knows—
Knows all the books, and nothing knows beside.
There is no Earth in her celestial form,—
Surpassing all of earthly loveliness
As luna's smile dim twinkle of a star;
Haloes of glory sparkle from her brow,—
In flash of eyes is Inspiration seen,
As seems entire made up of Angel-smiles!
Her length of wing expanded, rainbows skies,—
Soars stars, and looks with eyes undimm'd on Heaven,
As Eagle gazes on a noon-day sun:
Renown and Fame ride on her star-spread wing
And lead direct to Immortality.

True Genius soars with bright Enthusiasm
And makes all day where Learning's eye is night,
And wide Sahara is where she is not.
Bold Genius hath no orbit of her own,
But takes her way thro' heaven pell-mell across
Each star and Planet's path in universe—
A flaming comet firing all the sky,
And Wisdom stands wild-eyed as she sweeps by:
The Thunder-storm is noticed and revered,
While gentle Breezes pass unheeded on;
All see the Whirlwind humbling Forest's pride,
But Zephyrus flits unperceived away;
The lake is seen, while streams are lost in her,—
Let Pestilence abroad, and mankind quake;
So, mighty Genius—rarest gift of God!
Sweeps Earth storm-like and hath the thunder's roar:—
She plays with Lightning in his hell-fire den
And plucks high inspiration from his wing,
While Common-place like fire-fly, specks the night.

Bright Genius' wing is wild, and free as wild;
If shackel'd, she is Genius then no more:
Her wing is chain'd with Criticism's whims;
She dies 'neath Slavery's lash and Servitude—
Death-darts thro' heart of a Divinity!
But let the Goddess burst from rules of Art,
(By Dullness forged to bind old fogy Sense,)
Thro' fetters break as Samson broke from withs,
And soar to Fairy-land free and unchain'd

'Bove Wisdom's empire and the realm of Mind
By her own bright Invention deified,
Or Earth will dust her vision blind as bat's
And turn the Seraph to an empty Ghost
Sleep-graved with Common-place—forgotten quite.

Let Science, Knowledge, Wisdom, Learning all,
On weaker pinions flutter nearer Earth,
And talk to Common-place by rules of Art,
Or they shall find God's throne is not their home,—
The Eagle's flight 's presumption to the goose!
The cock, on his own dunghill crows at will,
While Eagle's proper home is the blue heaven—
A heaven above Poll's parlor-fanning wing.
Bright Genius glows like Moses' face on mount
While heaven'd with near approach of Deity;
But Critics, Israel-like, would have her vail'd—
Hide all the heaven bat-eyes can not behold,
Then, make her up according to their wills,
A thing of Earth, earthy as Earth they love,—
Rob Inspiration's robe of Glory's fires,
And shroud bright Immortality in dust
To make her like-mortality with them;
Impious hands would pluck her wing of heaven,—
Harness her wing'd Pegasus to the plow—
A drudge and stupid dullness turn for life,
And make him jog ass-like o'er plain turnpike
Subject to boy's GEEHO! or grannam's lash,
And then despise him—*for a poltry hack!*

But, Genius will to native Heaven in spite,
And take unearthly flights thro' Angel-bowers
Arms-link'd with her heart's love Enthusiasm,
And Eden Earth with Beatific Vision.

Imagination.

Imagination is archangel-brow'd,
And seraph-wing'd as Immortality.
Her wing celestial, is by soul spread out,
And leaves all temporal things as quick as thought,—
To light's remotest smile speeds on at will
And soars from world to infinite of worlds
Swift as the lightning, or the sunbeam's flight:
She flies throughout Existence in a thought,
With Chaos' shuddering darkness dwells at home,
And speaks to it God's own:—"Let there be light!"
Calls up at will her infinite of worlds—
Lifes them, and gives to each, light of her own,
And revels in the heart of Mystery!
She standeth on the verge where Nothing dwells
And sendeth on her eye sun-orb'd, soul-lit
To Chaos' womb of endless quietude
Beholding there new heavens in embryo!
Earth, Hell and Heaven of Heavens contain her not.
Thro' vast Eternity she flies alone
And scans Eternal things as those of Time—
Unvails those wonders to the eye of man,
And Fancy's Heaven fills with Divinities!

I said to her:—'*Ride up, and look on God!*'
But with affrighted stare, and wonder-smote
She quick returned with holy tremblings rent,
Whiles sacred Awe, and Silence cloven-tongued
Look'd from her death-seal'd lips—*Eternal things,*
That Heaven's nomenclature alone could name,
And less than Gabriel's trump might not announce,—
Ah! unrevealed to time, let them remain.

Eloquence.

"Whose words all ears took captive."—SHAKSPEARE.

God of the flowery speech—loved *Eloquence*—
Promethean fire upon the tongues of men!
Thy voice is sweet, thy words as honey flow—
A sweeter breath Arabia never breath'd!
A heavenly limberness of tongue sublim'd
That paints to life the picture of a thought
With charms celestial that set Earth on fire.
His sin-approving look proclaims—'*God's messenger,*'
While Feeling, every-tongu'd, speaks from his face,
And looks a lecture e'er lips speak a word!
Each eye is fix'd upon this man from God—
Attention's ear wide ope athirst to hear,
And every soul to drink instruction in.
He speaks! His speech is soul thrown out to soul;
His words, like burning arrows fire the heart,—
Seraphic sounds are echoes on the air,
And spirits quake as tho' a god had spoken!

His gestures talk from toes to finger's ends
Ten thousand-voic'd; his actions speak all o'er—
Speak out aloud like cloven tongues of fire
" *The wing of Passion, sentiment of heart!*"

The store-house of his mind celestial fill'd,
He soars above the common-place of things
As eagle towers above the fogs of Earth
To love the unvail'd face of smiling Heaven
And drink the glory from her noon-bright beams!
The mists of Earth shroud not his spirit's eye,
But 'yond all gloom he looks full-fac'd on Day
Aflame on throne of Zenith altitude,
And plucks bright Knowledge from the fount Divine
While world of Mind illumes with his God-light.
His speech, is gem'd with diamond-like remark,
And Music has her throne upon his tongue;
His words are like the voice of oracles,
While soul of feeling seems of tears compos'd.
Immortal thoughts roll ponderous thro' his brain
And leap as giants mighty from his tongue,
And all Earth-shaking in their Eloquence,
That take Mankind a captive at his will
And hang the world spell-bound upon his lip!
His theme, lies warm upon the speaker's heart;
Each thought 's a fire, and word a thunderbolt,—
Voice from the wilderness—Elijah's own!

He stops full oft with his emphatic words,
And heaven-full heart shuts up the gates of speech

While his soul-pictur'd face deep Passion burns,—
Looks all his thoughts and lets soul utter them,
And very silence speaks:—'*Language of soul*,'—
A silence far more eloquent than tongues!
His *Pauses* are—soul pouring out herself—
Spirit-sublimity revealing Heaven,
Where Passion shows her cloven tongue of fire
Beyond all power of language to express,
Or compass of all words to parallel—
'Yond Heaven-tip'd tongue to yield its thunderbolt!

Persuasion, Reason, dwell upon his tongue,—
His reasons weighty as the mountains are,
And they are hard to kick against as rocks.
He gives sunshine to dark Conjecture's gloom
Till wilderness of dun Obscurity
Is all illum'd by Heaven's celestial smile
And Godless Chaos wakes up—light and life.
Guilt stands transfix'd by tongue of Eloquence,
While Logic, double-edged smites Crime to heart,
And Sin is all confusion and alarm:—
Lays Falsehood on Truth's scales, and—*wanting* finds,
Sifts Ignorance till she flies away in wind;
Shows Superstition's eye—a hoodwink'd fool,
And casts from Error's heart—Beelzabub!
His argument, smites killingly to Sin,
Whiles Certitude, kings throne of skeptic Doubt,
And hurls blind Infidelity to Hell.
The thronging Nations wonder and admire
While sacred Truth and Demonstration clear

Reveal the dragon-wilds of Mystery,
And noonday, flames from face of Argument.
His mind, light-full as soul with Holy Ghost,—
Light, rays thro' soul like glory round a shrine—
An atmosphere of day to 'lume mind-night
And hold the hearts of hearers in his hand
Till each soul wakes to feel and know the truth—
Heaven-freedom from the servitude of Hell!
Blest Innocence applauds with loud amens,
And Echo's shouts are answers in the skies.

Memory.

The golden key to treasure-house of Mind
That opes the gate of huge Eternity,
And brings out hidden treasures new and old.
God-light that days the holy place of soul,
And resurrection gives to dust of Eld—
To shadows oned with void Oblivion.
Mind's ocean-depth where Understanding dwells,
And soul reveals her immortality;
An Usher to great lumber-room of Facts,
That scans Eternal things as tho' they were,—
To Present-time gives bald Antiquity,
And opes to mortals blank Eternity.
She speaks to mighty Past:—'*Arise and live!*'
And death-seal'd Past to living Present wakes
To reign god-lights in heaven of great Renown—
Angels of Fame and Immortality!

Religion.

O! what is this that wakes the soul
To ecstacy divine,
To taste the joys of Paradise
While flesh and blood enshrine?

It is RELIGION,—heavenly guest!
That tak'st from Death his sting,—
That giveth Faith her diamond eye
And Hope her flowr'y wing.

Say, how was she to mortals given—
By what great hand divine?
This light of life—this joy of heaven—
Celestial peace of mind!

'T was by the all-atoning Lamb—
Atonement large and free!
By Jesus' blood that freely bought
Our pardon on the tree.

Christ sent this Comforter from Heaven—
Full Paradise below!
And all the joys that are divine
In this bright Eden flow.

Without this Holy Comforter,
Man's spirit 's lost for aye;
For, soul is "dead in sin," and dead
To all eternity.

This Paraclete speaks to the soul :—
'*Be born to heavenly day!*'
And soul that Sin hath slain, is lifed
With—Immortality.

All must embrace Religion then
That would to Heaven aspire,
Or ever-dying souls shall die
In Lake that burns with fire.

But, some in sleep, fell Sin hath lock'd,
So deeply sunk in mire,—
That one dread plunge shall scarce awake
In Hell's eternal fire!

The Infant.

Couch'd on its Mother's breast, and bedded like
A star in Heaven, a rosy *Infant* lay,
On soft caresses and sweet kisses fed,—
Heart-joy and a full feast by night and day!
A laughing Beauty wed to Mother's love,
And smiling back maternal Love's caress,—
Young Innocence with look as bright as flowers!
One little foot, peeps 'neath its careless robe,
And lies—a soft snow-flake, down-drop'd from cloud.
Its classic-molded, Fairy-face of charms
All dotted o'er by dimples and sweet smiles,
Talks meaningly of Eden e'er its fall,—
A living Virtue—breathing Innocence—
Love's gem, and Mother's only ornament.

Twain Shall be One.—(*Holy Writ.*)

Our life 's one chaos of confusion all—
One somber night and lonely as the pall,
Till *Love*, broods o'er the waste of ruin dire,
And wakes up day and gives the heavenly fire
To banish darkness from the soul away
And open there—Life's Eden-ecstasy.
All hearts are void that have not found their love,
And they shall mourn their lost like widow'd dove:—
One desert-wild, wide opening in the breast,
Deprives of peace, and robs the soul of rest.
Unwedded Man, is lost without his mate,—
Breaks Nature's laws and fix'd decrees of Fate;
While those united into perfect Love
Have sip of joy from Angel-bliss above.

Suspicion.

Suspicion 's a pale-pausing Restlessness,—
She 's the sly-creeping serpent of the mind—
A living Jealousy stuck full of eyes!
Suspecting *all things* are not what they *seem;*
She thinks she spies defects in Virtue's self,
And dreams of mites that never had a name.
Suspicion, changes Possibility
To Probability, then oft ripes all
To Certainty, and holds Chance fix'd as Fate.
She 's ever poor, least Want *might* haunt her door—

A *fancied* Wretchedness that 's *truly* wretch'd,—
In misery *now*, for fear of woes—to *come!*
With future evils fills Life's cup with gall
To desolate bright Eden e'er its fall!

The Egotist.

He 's curs'd with an incurable disease
Call'd the 'Bighead!' His eye (he is all I)
Sees nothing else on Earth but self alone,
Or all mankind as emmets in his path!
He thinks creation is complete in him,
And Earth was made eight thousand miles across
To give him room to spread his vanity!
He shows his peacock-feathers to the sun
With head toss'd six feet high above his boots—
Pride swell'd and dropsy-like, skin-burstingly!
Almighty-bull of all Earth's woods, is he.

Niagara.

Composed while standing on the extreme verge of Table Rock.

I long'd to see thee from a very child,
And do I now behold thee face to face,
Applause of Earth and wonder of the world,
Where Nature dwells with her Beatitudes
Clad in her rainbow-robe and ghost-like Mist?
A Mist, made up entire of hovering Ghosts

To hide a Deity from mortal sight!
I look on thee as on a sacred thing,—
A revelation from the Fairy-world,
Ay, Fairy-Land before enraptured vision
Soul-feasting as a dream of Paradise!

Enchantment worthy of the Fairy-isles—
The sight noons out and smites me like a blow!
I stand with Awe, and respiration 's gone,
To give me soul and body to the scene,—
To see Magnificence excel herself
And glory of Dream-land made visible!
By roar of waters, heart-enchanted—lost
As if a Syren's song hath captur'd sense,
And made immortal Mind her prisoner,—
Soul-fix'd to her as needle to its pole—
In spell-bound frenzy quite Niagarized!

I see God in thy face, and bow the knee:—
My eye's idolatry long and profound,
Is it the voice of God thy waters speak?
Don't say me—'*Nay!*' or I'll believe it jest—
But answer—'*Yea!*' for well I know it truth.
A foamy orator art thou Niagara,
Whose roar eternal, thunder-toned speaks—'GOD!"
The very mouth of God-made Nature—thou,
To send Truth home to Infidelity
Proclaiming 'GOD!" with everlasting roar.
God, laid his mighty hand upon thy brow,
And impress of that Hand's still visible;

He put His finger in the heart of Earth,
And scoop'd Niagara out from Lake to Lake,
And lo! its shores were walls of adamant!
Stay! I must cast the sandals from my feet,
For this is holy ground—a God is near,—
Lo! Earth, as Aspen-leaf, quakes miles around!
When God shall speak with Judgment-trumpet-voice
Mortality's death-slumbering dust to wake—
"ARISE YE DEAD, AND FORTH TO JUDGMENT COME!"
Will that voice be like thine—Niagara?

Those falling waters fall forever more,
White-flashing in their foam and brilliancy,—
A Fateful rush of wild despair, that comes
With frenzied leap all frothing into air—
An Ocean-leap from off a precipice!
Destraction's rush that terrifies the soul
Down-thundering to heart-center of the Earth!
A chaos of mad waters tumbling down
In frightful awfulness of a death-bound
With headlong fury and a world-crash fall—
Fell Desperation's leap and the Hell-plunge!
Till burden'd Air is but one jarring sound,
One everlasting and romantic roar—
A roar of waters and a world of spray!
The murderous Cataract afoam with rage,
Leaps ever from Niagara's awful brow
As furious lion bounding on his prey;
While fallen waters grow like mountains up
To meet her desperate coming in mid air,

And god-like armies join in hideous crash,
Whiles Rage and Fury in death-struggle, foam.
Outrageous waters leap with Maelstrom-bound
Up from their deep-dug graves like maniacs,
And with down-dashing floods contend with might,
And battle to the death for victory.
Surge-army meets Surge-army, and devours,
And Billow tumbles Billow down to death.
Still, mountain Billows rise Olympus-high,
By falling Billows met ten-millions-tunn'd
That dash to foam and bubbles at a blow;
When, all, down sink by Whirlpool's heart engulf'd
Till metamorphos'd by that Hadean-whirl
Mad floods rise up—a River in its strength
That flies an arrow swifting to a Lake.
Uproarous floods rage, swell, boil, froth and foam,
And in death-struggles whirl with bedlam-roar
Whose rumbling thunder, booms eternal on—
The roar of waters in death-agonies!
Niagara's horror-roar, seems not of Earth,—
As if Eternity hath found a voice,
And unto awe-struck ear of Time reveals
Some wonder-mystery of a Deity:—
Like Horror's voice, or Hell's far off uproar.
An aqueous Epic for the World's charm'd eye
To gaze at and admire till Time 's no more;
'T is Water's Iliad till Judgment-day,—
A Battle-wonder 'yond a Homer's dream:—
'Yond ancient gods in all their fury join'd,
Tho' in the strife of their almightiness

They rend the pavement of the pagan-heaven
Till Jove's throne falls to pieces like a dream!

What clouds of Spray arise—the spectral Ghosts
Of all that dash-to-death-down-tumbling sea!
Dank, airy, curling, wreathing into Mist—
Chaotic-wild-bewilderment of Mist
Uprising like the smoke of Erebus,
And just the thing God makes the raincloud of!
Eye-blinding Spray, down falls in ceaseless showers—
Thick-white-outbreathings of the Cataract
All rainbows-gem'd—so many smiles of Heaven!
It seems to me, Heaven's rainbow 'round the brow
Of an eternity of Spirits bless'd,
And yet, a rainbow-brow'd Reality:—
Hot-breathings of some tortured Deity
Whom Jove in his soul-blasting ire hath chain'd
And now astruggle with Hell-agony.

The greatest glory that the hand Divine
Made this side Heaven,—thou art what God can do!
A complete glory that takes hold of soul,
And bids her cast her sandals from her feet
And tiptoe stand—white-eyed Astonishment
By Awe and Fascination spell-bound held:—
The thought of thy unique sublimity
Shall add fresh glories to all coming life,
And quite divine thy every-loveliness.
I wonder much, if it's profane to ask:—
Will Paradise a full-perfection be
Unless Life River hath a rainbow-clad

Cascade, just like thine own—Niagara?
Is Heaven complete without Niagara?
Then, we will have one near our Father's house,—
But can it be more beautiful than thee—
World-wonder-charm to every eye that sees?
For thou art what Omnipotence can do,—
No hand but God's could make Niagara:
O! thou wilt do to be translated *there*,
For thou 'rt near a spirituality—
Much less of Time than of Eternity,—
The thing that Happiness can say '*Enough*' to
When she hath seen the face of her Beloved
That wakes the soul up—Immortality!
And—stay! my very spirit in me leaps,
To know if the Creator did not say:—
'COME NOW, AND LET US MAKE NIAGARA!'
'A God-made work,' thy every voice declares;
And sure, the great Omnipotence in might,
To try what His almighty hand could do,
Grasp'd Chaos' heart, and made Niagara—
Time's wonder and the Hell of Waters—*was*.

Muse! wilt thou not awake thy song of heaven?
Why is not every word I speak, a poem,
When inspiration 's felt, and visible?
Behold! the Muses dumb and silent stand,
Trembling in presence of a Deity!
Sweet Poesy, becomes a common-place,
Bright Romance too—all nothingness to *this*.
Painting, lets rainbows-making pencil fall,

While mind-convincing and converting Eloquence,
With Romance, Sculpture, find it sacred ground,
And cloth'd upon by mum Astonishment,
Stand, soul-adoring with divinest Awe
That feels it a profanity to speak.
Exaggeration's heavens-outdoing self,
Takes his own brain-bewilder'd summerset
Off foamy brink of frightful Cataract
With Sam Patch leap to infinite below,
And vanishing in misty nothingness,
With death-sigh owns :—'*I have no being here!*'
E'en sacred Truth, is tongueless infancy,—
Owns with knee-bent humility of soul :—
'The dictionary is unpublished yet—
Language unspoken by the tongues of men,
That can describe Niagara's awful front,
Or thunder, like that water-precipice,
Whose sea-down-dashing-crush, shakes Earth's great heart,
As Earthquake, the world's soul, to central fires.'

The soul may feel, but Painting may not paint,
Nor Song daguerreotype that aqueous Fall
That looks a Dream more than Reality,—
A Picture-wonder to all-coming Time
Eternal-rainbows-crown'd and clad in spray!
A Raphael, would let his pencil fall,—
Soul-lost in presence-chamber of his God!
And Orpheus, that moved the very rocks,
And awed wild beasts, as Silence' statue stand,

Or harp, discordant-tun'd, give jargon to the air,—
Too great a glory for Art's hand to grasp,
Or less than Nature's self to parallel—
Nay, Nature hath but one Niagara!
Let earthly greatness stand upon thy brink
And sigh out truth:—'Lo! I a nothing am!'
Leviathan, with river in his mouth—
The greatest wonder of the works of God,
Would float a speck on thy down-tumbling sea,
And with a heart-feel say:—'I'm but a mite.'
Enough! I'm oned with thee while oned with Life,
And when all-conquering Death shall throw his dart,
He'll find thy name, Niagara, on my heart.

Conscience.

The prompter in Life's drama, *Conscience* is,
An inward bible and the spirit's light
That tells us how to act our parts aright;
A sacred judge and inward monitor,—
Throne of the soul where all the Virtues dwell
To weigh Man's deeds from cradle to the grave;
Fair Virtue's court, that self to trial brings
And shows what Evil is, and what is good.
Lamp of the Lord illuming Mortal-night,—
Ay, Conscience is, God-light in soul of Man—
God's own handwriting on the book of mind,
And eye of soul proclaiming good and ill—
Both good and evil teaching Man to know.

In Conscience's mirror 's seen the face of Heaven:
A conscience pure, is peaceful quietude,—
In very cannon's mouth may sleep secure,
Unharm'd by all the powers of Earth and Hell;
While guilty-conscience is, life's purgatory,—
An imp snake-tongued, with virus in his tooth
Sore-rending spirit with the sting of Hell.

The Fool.

See Folly's child, brought up by Ignorance;
He tosses high his empty head in air
(Things light do float while heavy bodies sink)
Without a mind, to wag his tongue aright!
He is an all-tongued impudence and shame;
He talks forever, and he nothing says—
Gabs nothings and much nonsense in an hour!
Silence, to Fool, would be sage Wisdom's crown,—
To him, the rod would—weight of knowledge give.
He shows his tongue, to show his lack of sense,—
'T would take some scores of fools to make one man!
His infant-mind 's mask'd in the shroud of night,—
The Spirit did not brood upon the '*Fool*,'
And God's—'*Let there be light*," was not to him.

The Babes.

With cheek of flowers sun-bright with cheerfulness,
A youthful Mother smil'd upon her *Babes*,—
Two laughing Beauties fair as Innocence,
That look'd the Angel-forms that haunt our dreams—

Sweet Innocence's repose on Virtue's breast!
Their little, classic-molded cheeks of morn
By love-smiles lit and dimple-spotted o'er
Talk meaningly—heart-feast by day and night—
A world of joy, song, grace and loveliness!
With what maternal fondness doth she hang
Lost o'er her soul-loved charge—the darling ones!
Heart-dancing time that brims Life's cup with bliss—
That Mother wooing Innocence to dreams,
Lost to herself and dwelling in her *Babes!*

Man.

When fierce wolves howl let antelopes beware,
And the wild ox avoid the hungry bear;
The King of beasts a flying deer pursues,
Or takes his royal feast on kangaroos;
But these from kin, will quickly turn aside—
(A beast by brother beast hath seldom died),
Hyenas fierce, hyenas shrink to kill,—
Tigers refuse their brother's blood to spill:—
But ah! let *trumpets sound*—the war-horse neigh,
Then *Man meets Man*—in horrible array!
While cannons roar and trembling banners play—
Man sheds his brother's blood in open day!
Yes—Man! at fellow Man, will throw his dart,
And laugh to see it quiver in his heart!

Both Men and Devils 'like are ever fools,
Folly, alike, their actions also, rules;

DESTRUCTION, is their Empire and renown,—
Kingdoms to win by *blood*, and wear a crown!
So, Popery thought, and Inquisitions fell
Spread out wide havoc with the hate of Hell!
But where his Empire now, and where his reign,
When Babylon hath fallen and Beast slain?
Him, Virtue killed by *love*, for murderers pray'd—
Drop'd tears for Persecution while he slay'd!
Her Eden-reign is—*blessedness and peace*,
And tho' Heaven pass, her Kingdom shall not cease.
God, governs by this golden axiom true:—
LOVE CONQUERS ALL, AND MERCY SHALL SUBDUE.

Envy.

Envy! the fiend of Hell that loves her mire,
And aims to stab bright Glory to the heart,—
A pamper'd demon smiting Peace in twain!
Her tongue is poisons-tipp'd, down-dropping bane
And hissing blasts from lowest Erebus—
The eye of Evil and the sting of Death!
With jaundic'd eye askance, she looks at Worth,
And sickens when Perfection she beholds,—
Grows sick to see superior Excellence
Above her rise, and dares to live—a man.
Base Envy, is the hound that barks at Name—
Hell-hound that bites both Affluence and Renown,
Snapping at all things greater than herself,
And seeks to rise by pulling Greatness down!

She spits her ratsbane-gorge on Honor's brow—
That Godlike weight of Kingly royalty!
Blest Innocence, is Guilt, at Envy's bar,
And Piety, a martyr at her stake.
With slander's cat-o'-nine-tail lash in hand
Steep'd in the loathsome adder's poisonous bane,
She smiteth Fame and Fortune right and left,
And gores the sacred heart of Character,
Till Wisdom, Virtue, bleed at every pore,
And their pure souls with plaudits reach the skies.

Inhumanity.

The moans of pining Penury and Want
Melt not the heart of *Inhumanity:*—
There 's flint around that ice-cold den of hate
That Love's bright smiles can not imparadise,—
In his hell-heart live Satan and his imps!
His acts of inhumanity and death
Sent his aged parents mourning to their graves.
His ear is deaf to widow's wail of woe,—
One who could rob the orphan of his crumb
And dig the dead man from his sepulcher—
Earth's tear of blood and groan of agony!
I measure the inhuman demon in
His breast, by his infernal acts to man,
And find wherein he lacks of being all
Devil, is made of base brutality—
A monster without head and likewise heart!

The foulest blot on Human Nature's page;
The whitest spot in him 's cimmerian—
Sear'd down to depths by Old Iniquity.
In bosom's furnace burn volcanic fires;
In this vile sin, Revenge and Murder dwell—
Death in his words, and murder all his thoughts!
His deeds of blood, fell Cruelty surpass,
And give a horror to the name of fiend:—
He doth out-knave Old Knavery and Crime
And a dishonor is to Degradation—
I measure Old Apollyon by this man!

Slander.

His sulphurous breath is as the fumes of Hell;
He spits his poison on the works of God—
Gnashing fiend-fangs in open eye of day!
A flying Dragon brooding on Death-wings
To blot the sun from universe of God;
A vile reviler of both God and man,—
Counts others faults but e'er forgets his own.
His tongue 's malevolence and poisons-tipp'd;
He is the murderer of Character,
And strives by day and night to hurl Renown,
Worth, Wisdom, Honor, Genius, all headlong
To Shame and everlasting Infamy,
Where grim Forgetfulness gapes out ghost-grins
At dark Oblivion and Nonentity.

Avarice.

Her famish'd father was a prowling wolf,
Her dam a Griffin, born in Dragon's den,
And nurs'd by Hydra in a Satyr's cave.
Starvation is the home wherein she dwells;
Want, Poverty, hang round her all their rags,
And Hunger looks from famin'd *Avarice.*
Tho' ever feasting, she ne'er feasted is!
She stores her gains and is not satisfied—
Possessing all things yet complains of want,
Because she loves my purse more than her own.
If Ophir's bank were hers, she 'd want Peru's,—
Nay, give her all the world, she still would weep
That it was dust—not made of solid gold!
Yea, fill each wish her grasping heart can name,
She 'd die of grief to find—*that it was all!*
She hath a greedy devil at the heart
That grasps at shadows to let substance fall:—
She 'd sooner fill her coffers with gold dust
Than her dark mind with Wisdom's sacred light,
Or heart, with all the virtues under Heaven.
Canst satisfy the soul with temporal things?
'T is counting sands and drinking oceans dry!

Pride.

See empty headed, devil-hearted—*Pride!*
The whelp of Vanity, base Folly's brat
Bred up by Sin and nursed in heart of fools—
An air-blown bubble full of empty self!

His lofty look, down showers hopes-blasting Scorn
On passing Poverty in honest rags.
This stately-stepping son of Lucifer,
Rattling with starch and ruffles struts along
With a ten-million-pounds of pompousness
Without two cents to jingle in his purse,
And thinks his own god-rivaling self enough
To fill the vast world with himself alone!
High flies his plume of pride aspiring Heaven,
And great his wonder why the rabble live
To cross his path—*when Earth was made for him!*

Revenge.

Pride, upon Cruelty, begat—*Revenge:*
Forthwith from baneful quagmire he arose,—
Imps on his horrid hair hung shrieking deaths,
And from his combin'd locks fire-serpents hiss'd
While thunders of his brow announc'd—'THE FIEND!'
His tatter'd garments all disordered, foul,
Stream round like many flames round damned Ghosts
And ill conceal Deformity within.
In snaky-bosom's den, and all unsheath'd,
Revengeful poniards pant for blood of foes.
His foot is cloven, and his head of horns
Contraction is, and forehead low as Sin's.
He is flame-breath'd as Pandemonium,
And sulphur-mouth'd as the infernal pit—
Kindlings of Hell in his fierce eyebeams burn!

His desperate grin hath a cold death in it—
His fiend-like visage nests an Erebus!

Untutor'd Justice, fiery Vengeance is
With a fork'd tongue steep'd in iniquity;
His soul 's a boiling Rage—a burning wrath,
And heart of hate is the heart's hate of Hell;
His own heart's venom is his daily food,
And every word 's a dagger poison-tipt.

Fear.

Fear sits the heart-strings and the soul a-dance,
And whets the mind keen as the razor's edge.
Her cautious eyes white-rolling, take in ghosts,
And fiends and spectres meet her every view;
Her eye doth magnify ten thousand times,
Mole-hills to mountains round about her rise,
Till Fancy's goblins seem realities,
And her wan visage stares out like a Death!
Thro' her half-open lips, gleam chattering teeth,—
Thoughts wild, and storm and tumult is her breast,
And hair like quills on back of porcupine.
A corpse-like Paleness gaping like a Ghost
Tiptoe and breathless—trembling in her place,
And palsied at the noise her garments made!
Of quicksilver, her spirit 's all composed,
And fainting body made of aspen-leaf.
Her failing limbs quake 'neath her while she stands—
An ague-shaking and a white-lipp'd *Fear*

Whose heart forever lodges in her throat!
She seeks to wrap her in grim Darkness' robe
And shuns the light as worst of enemies,—
Sight-loosing foot outflies the winged winds!

Anger.

Fell Anger looks a hot Beelzebub,
Fiend-likeness and the image of an Imp!
His firm-set joints a trembling Eagerness,
And foot of wind hath an elastic step.
Distracted features, and eyes all a-glare,
Picture Deformity defying Hell.
His vengeful eyes, are daggers, and they stab,—
Their fiery flames flash out death-arrows barb'd;
In their wrath-fires a native demon dwells
And madden'd spirit dens therein, lightning—
Eye-glaring Vengeance set on fire of Hell!
A very fiend at heart, and madman-brain'd,
And his wrath-face,heart's thirst for vengeance speaks,
Storm-brow'd, clench-fisted, Devil-hearted Rage!
Teeth set, blue lips part ope, with mad dog snarls,
And hot and hurried breathing is a storm,—
Breathing red-hot-hell-fires of human wrath!
With full-fill'd heart and swell'd-to-bursting veins
He raves and foams like lion robb'd of prey—
Dread monster to all enemies around
That seeks to eat his foes up bodily.
He steeps his tongue in Venom's fount of gall,

And fills his soul with dreadful Fury's bane;
His squeak-voice utters broken sentences
In accents false and hurried utterance.
All evil Passions are Hell's battering rams
That hurl down Life's clay tenement to dust,
And o'er these Hell-hounds vile, reigns Anger, chief—
Fiend-claw'd, and hottest devil of them all.

Give Anger sway, and he'll devour himself,
But hedge him in, and he'll seek for thy life.
Subdue thy rage, or be by Rage subdued—
Wrath whets a sword to gore thee to thy heart.
Fierce Anger 's found in the fool's heart alone,
While Peace and Love 's enthron'd on Wisdom's soul.
Fell Anger desolates the soul of man,
Robs Reason of its gem and Judgment slays,—
Face of a Demon to an Angel gives,
And turns all hearts to furies, ripe for Hell.

True Ambition.

Swell not with pride, vain mortal, here below,
By pride, the Devil fell—thy constant foe;
But cease thy murmurings and thy sour complaints,
They very ill become the mouth of saints,
And leave to Folly—Hell's own brainless flirt
And peacock's tail to dabble in the dirt.
Ah! should frail Man be proud, a mortal boast,
When he 's but dust, corrupt and fallen—lost?

Canst prop with puny arm old Ocean's head,
Or drag Leviathan out with hook of lead?
Then mount, aloft Religion's heavenly wings
And soar with Virtue to the King of Kings;
Less flight, is Immortality's disgrace,
And this alone—*Life's golden, glorious race.*

Trust Earth! Are not the joys of Earth too few
To call this world—'A Paradise below?'
Do not Earth-pleasures die as soon as born,
And airy robed Bliss fade with the Morn?
Doth rosy Hope not smile with promise fair,
To shower on us the tempests of despair?
Can we spend life on downy beds of ease,
Or, 'scape the woful family of Disease?
'*No!*' Wisdom cries—'O! leave the land of Nod,
Let earthly pleasures go, and look to God:—
O! mount aloft 'bove vanities of earth,
Leave them to Folly, Pride and Sin and Mirth,
And *righteous live*, live for—eternal rest,
And thou shalt live—Earth's, Heaven's supremely
bless'd.'

We all do fade as a Leaf.—(*Holy Writ.*)

Can there be aught that 's stable upon Earth
When she herself is daily turning round?
All earthly joys do wither soon as grasp'd;
The nimble Hours dance little lives away,
And we are old e'er we have learn'd to live;
The rose, soon lays her crimson beauty by,

And fairest ones the soonest do depart.
Man 's man tho' he on air balloons rides heaven;
Yea, strength shall flee away from giant's arm,
And Kings turn back to dust tho' they're embalm'd.
Our life's short day soon turns to a long night;
From Life's pathway, all stumble to the tomb—
We 're mourners at the funerals of our friends.
Frail Nature cries—'Age must give place to youth;'
Upon his father's grave as on a stage
The son plays Life's great drama to the end;
Death throws Life's playthings by, and bids man sleep,
He breathes on us, and we're—dust of a tomb!

All things must die and turn to dust again
Fast as Life's flight can hurry them to tombs,
For 'MORTAL 's' written on the face of all,
And FINIS ends the mighty Book of Time.
All things do flourish, fade, and pass away;
We die, and others live to weep our fall,
And fall themselves in turn, a few days hence:
The light of life but guides one's steps to death,
And all do live but to prepare their tomb.

Life, but a preparation is for Death;—
Then give each moment of thy life to God,
And make thy treasure-house Eternity.
Seek Virtue more than life and all Earth's stores;
Wed Piety, and hold Religion fast;
They're diamonds when the finest gold grows dim:—
These gems alone are current in the skies,

When all else fail, they shall but brighter grow,
And star thy crown when stars themselves shall fall,
To shine thy glories thro' the Heaven of Heavens.

The Grave.

All-conquering Grave—creation's final home!
Clay-house, where Earth receives her dust again,
Thy jaws are ope for Old Mortality!
Thou drinkest up the mourner's falling tears,
Nor pity nor compassion dwells with thee:
Thou art as inexorable as Death,
And Life and Time must fall and sleep with thee,—
Great Being's last bedchamber is the *Grave.*
A solemn pause on the Eternal-brink
Sleep-lock'd and quite beyond the vale of Dreams—
A long, lone bed of dreamless quietude
Where the soul's mantle falls to sleep in peace.
Thy silence speaks to very heart of Life
With awful power and deep solemnity
Of Judgment-trump by Hierarch Angel blown:—
Thou turn'st to awe the very heart of Hate
And wrappest Envy in her winding sheet.
Solemnities hang round thee like a pall,
And thy midnight is dark as Mystery—
Sublime the quiet of the lonely GRAVE!
Death-brink, and threshold of Eternity,—
Night-lifeless, frown'd on by Oblivion,
Where Grim Death holds his carnival of worms.

Thy calm, lone, fearful night seems long—how long!
But worn-out Nature needeth long repose,
Well suited to wretch'd Feebleness and Age—
Sweet peace and rest from toil and every ill;
One long, lone night, but Morning shall arise
And slumber wake refresh'd from all Life's woes.
Sin dreads the dark, and Folly fears the Grave,
While Virtue's eye of faith sees God beyond
And fears the tomb as little as her bed.
Death's downy couch art thou—care-killing Grave!
Where we put off Mortality's vile robe
Cloth'd on with Immortality and Heaven—
Thy opening is Heaven's welcome to the soul.
The quiet Grave, is but a dressing-room
Where we poor mortals lay Corruption by
And put the robes of Incorruption on
To see the Bridegroom married to the Bride.
The very portal of Eternity,—
Our safe way home to heavenly Father's house,
For Heaven is seen dim-dawning through thy shades,
And day Eternal opes all round the tomb,
From which the Just will rise to sleep no more
When Morning wakes to—Immortality.

Time.

Time, is, the mettle of which Life is made,
Seed-time for harvest of Eternity,—
It is the nursery of Eternity,
Probation's stage where Life 's on trial kept,—

'T is Immortality's minority
Rip'ning for the inheritance eterne—
Apprenticeship that traineth for the skies.
Sure, Time, duration in progression is,
It is duration measur'd, parcel'd out—
The morning's dawn to an eternal day.
Time is Existence's constant flowing stream
Forever emptying yet forever full.
Life's lamp to light us to Eternity;
Life's journey to the center of all Being,
A broken link in Being's endless chain—
A fragment from Eternal Being broke.
Fleet-flying Time, an isthmus is that joins
Eternity to vast Eternity;
A day of grace allowed Mortality
To put the white robe of Salvation on.

Time plucks the rose from cheek of Loveliness,
And dims the day that lights up Beauty's eye;
Time blasts the sweetest flowers that bloom on earth,
To wrinkles turns the dimpled face of youth,—
Blasts Joy, and withers every bliss on Earth,
And whets the dart that gives us to the tomb.
Time drives his steed to precipice of Death,—
His rolling years roll all things into dust,
And ripes Life's harvest for the sepulcher.
Time's clock strikes warnings for Mortality,
And bids Life for Eternity prepare,
While Echoes answer thousand-voic'd—'*Prepare!*'
Time's clock counts o'er Life's fickle moments all

To final one that snaps the fatal chord
And opes Eternity to spirit-sight.

Time flies, and his increase is Life's decrease,
The loss of time is loss of life to all,
And loss of life is—King of Terrors come,—
How short a span between us and our graves!
Years, Months, Weeks, Days, his nimble children are,
And on their lightning wings around him play
As Cupids round the fabled goddess' smiles
Thro' Life's short day to the eternal-night.
Fast-rolling Years, the quickly-passing Months,
The hasty-skipping Weeks, fleet-flying Hours
And lightning-winged Moments—each a scythe
Fatal as Death, and mows its thousands down.
From winged Moments learn how short is life
And value Heaven's own precious boon the more:—
Each moment is a sphere in Life's short hour,
And every time they ride their axles round
Ten thousand Mortals huddle to the grave!
So like the lightning is Time's rapid flight,
We backward gaze to look upon his wing,—
Haste, or be left eternally behind.
Unsearchable to man, to-morrow's fate,—
Ah! who can say—'To-morrow shall be mine?'

Sweet Time, that is so oft for baubles sold,
Or thrown away as thing of nothing worth,
The wealth of all the stars can not redeem.
Record of Time, the history is of Death;

Each day 's another page to book of Life,
And all men's actions there are register'd;—
Each moment spent, recorded is in Heaven,
Rewarded with eternal bliss or woe,—
My soul! mark thou the moments as they pass!

Eternity.

Eternity! Ah! who can measure thee—
Who count the years in vast Eternity?
From birth of Worlds to their old age and fall
Is but a cipher 'gainst Eternity.
The mighty Gabriel's flight thro' vast unknown
Since dawn of Time till Judgment trump shall sound
Would only find this axiom to be true:
Less than Eternity knows not Eternity.
When thrice ten million ages roll their years,
Eternal-clock moves not one moment on;
And this, infinituply multiplied,
The shadow stands upon the dial's face
Same as they stood e'er these had run their course!
To billions add as many trillions more;
To trillions add quadrillions twice the sum,
And unto this infinity itself,
'Tis still a unit to—*Eternity*,—
Forever and forever-more as far
From ending as beginning is—ETERNITY!
A billion billion rolling ages gone,
With billion billion centuries in their train,

And myriad myriads more in mighty march,
Yet, ever and the same the dial points
On and for aye to vast—Eternity,—
Points to Duration countless—*yet to come!*
One sea beyond all length, or width, or depth—
An ocean without bottom, end or coast!
Immeasurable, incomprehensible—
Without diameter, circumference!
An unbegun and endless evermore
Where times eternal roll eternal on,
And ages rolling on—forever roll
One everlasting NOW that knows no end,—
End of all ends without beginning—end!
Thou lifetime of my God—ETERNITY!
Omnipotence alone can fathom thee,
And only God, can fully comprehend.

One endless *present*, is Eternity,
Whose being, no past tense will ever know;
One boundless future, all—forever-more:—
No days, no months, no years—one living NOW,—
One everlasting, fix'd—ETERNAL NOW!

Incomprehensible Eternity!
The very name, wraps mind in world of thought,
And every thought hángs awed upon the word—
All lost as bubbles are on Ocean's width.
Time's end, and jubilee of Being all,
Duration boundless, endless infinite
Where none can say—'One moment hath gone by;"
Where centuries rolling on, forever roll,

While Angel-smiles light Heaven to always smile,
And Hell howls out to howl eternally:—
Thou lifetime of bless'd Immortality,
Thou mak'st Heaven, HEAVEN, and Hell a HELL
indeed!

END.

The Closing Scene.

A VISION—IN TWELVE BOOKS.

BY JAMES WOODMANSEE.

CINCINNATI:
PRINTED AND SOLD AT THE METHODIST BOOK CONCERN.

OPINIONS OF CRITICS.

I call the Closing Scene, the Paradise Lost of America.
SAMUEL ROGERS,
Author of "Pleasures of Memory."

The Closing Scene rivals the Divina Commedia of Dante.
THOMAS NOON TALFOURD,
Author of "Ion."

The Closing Scene is one flight of sublimity from beginning to end—awfully grand as Book of Job.
THOMAS EDWARDS,
Author of "Winter."

"The Closing Scene" is the only great Poem, America has produced, and it is one of the most wonderful in any language.
JOSEPH MAYHEW.

A New Poet.—Among the many new things of this age, is a new Poem by James Woodmansee,—an Epic in twelve books entitled—"The Closing Scene." The Author is not satisfied to be a mere story-telling rhymer, but employs the boldest strain of Poetic description; not occasional lovely gems scattered among profuse assemblages of insipid and drowsy lines—"dragging their slow length along," but a rapid succession of bold and original thoughts and comparisons.

REV. L. F. VAN CLEVE.

The Closing Scene.—A very able Poem. Woodmansee is not unknown to our readers; we have published some fine fugitive pieces from his pen.—[Boston Olive Branch.

"The Closing Scene" is one Picture-gallery of gorgeous Paintings. Every page is a picture original and wonderful, terrific or sublime, beautiful or picturesque, and all as brilliantly glorious as summer's sunshine. The richest book for the Painter or Sculptor that I have read, is—"The Closing Scene." What a Panorama would it not make if painted by an Angelo or a Raphael!—[Journal.

The Closing Scene: A Vision in Twelve Books. By J. Woodmansee.—We do not know anything of James Woodmansee only as we have seen his name connected with this book, but if others are as favorably struck with the beauty of expression and the sublimity of description of the "Closing Scene" as we are, he will not long remain in obscurity. The characters here presented are the noblest in the universe—God and Man—the scene of action—Time and Eternity. The book abounds in plain truths as well as beautiful descriptions. It reminds us of Pollock's "Course of Time" and also of Milton's great epic.—[Galesburg Democrat.

The Closing Scene evinces a terseness and vigor of style rare among modern authors.—[Eaton Register.

New Book.—Among the many recent publications, there is none that stands higher in point of beauty and sublimity, than the Closing Scene, a poem, written by James Woodmansee. The work shows the mark of deep thought and thorough study, and should be in the parlor or library of every family.—[Middletown Journal.

The New Poem.—Woodmansee is a lover of the horrible, and he is ever at home in the sublime and terrible. In terrible sublimity and horrible description, 'The Closing Scene' has no equal in any language, and its Second Book, in my judgment, is the sublimest book ever penned by man.

Though the Awful, is strictly Woodmansee's fort, nevertheless, he can come out of Pandemonium at will, and fling as wide the gates of Paradise, as ever they were flung by less than Angel-arm. To prove this, let the reader turn to Book V, page 201, and take a walk with him through Eden-bowers to page 222, and he will show himself as full of beauty as a rose. He that wishes to see the Picturesque and the Beautiful, sublimely mingled with the Melancholy and the Terrible, let him commence Book VI, and read to page 251, and if he does not own there are more Beauties of celestial loveliness here, than can be found in the same number of pages of any other Poet, I must say to that man—Judgment is wanting, and taste is bad indeed. Woodmansee's paintings of Nature are far richer than Thompson's, and his Picturesque is more divine than Tennyson's. To me, the pages above referred to, are all—the Picturesque in its perfection—if anything in this imperfect world can be perfect—they are *perfect.*

The *thoughts* of the Closing Scene are original, overwhelming and sublime. They all jump in the soul of things at once, and tell at once what Common Place would prate about for an hour. The following extract is composed of *single lines* picked here and there from our American Iliad, and like Heralds from Eternity they meet our wandering gaze.

"Despair's simoons spread desert through his soul.
Wasteful as Earthquake jail'd in womb of worlds.
Sahara was behind him as he fled.
Annihilation opening in its look.
The dust-awaking coming of the Lord.
Their virtue gives perfume unto their dust.
Soul-loosing as grim Death's dark Vale of Skulls.
His stride Apollyon's shaking Erebus.
More mighty than Xerxes five millions-arm'd.
Startling as crush of a mad cataract.
He look'd a prodigy—surprising Faith.
Dark-deep-dumb-dead-soul-smitings of Despair.
Bathed locks of long midnight in home of Mist.
With spectres damn'd red-sparkling in her skirts.
Worlds on fix'd orbs, ajar hung as he spake.
A Dragon's jargon mutter'd from his throat.
Through-seeing gaze read thought in embryo.
God's worldquake-coming and the great Assize.
He look'd upon the other side of things.
A world-consuming comet of a man.
All the Ten Plagues of Egypt in one man.
A fool's misdeeds are history of Crime.
His fame's a blot on temple of Renown.
To infamy on thro' the paths of Shame.
Chaotic Darkness storming from his face.
Bright Fancy's child 'lone equal'd by a god.
E'er God-lit Being throned a Deity.
A blazing sun in Wisdom's firmament.
The tomb to noon with present Deity.
Loud rattling many nothings in an hour.

Vile contradiction and a living lie.
Imagination's view of Deity.
Earth's heart doth hallow Virtue like a God.
Rub Life as cipher from the Book of Time.
One long unmeasur'd ruin in his length.
Sublimely speaking-grandeur-thrones of gods.
These are the heavens God made, and no star dimm'd.
Like many fires, pale Ghosts light up grave-yards.
Swings his Creation-uncreating-club.
He sweeps Hell-armied on dragon-wings.
Eternity dim-dawning thro' his form.
His goblin-face as grim gaunt Famine grinn'd.
And Palsy's smite fell on the face of things.
Reap Fallen Nature's harvest as a field.
I'll make wide deserts thro' the heart of Life.
A scythe that playeth like Archangel's wing.
That hell-crown'd King and giant-greatness—Death.
Chain-lightning telegraphs the storms approach.
Ghost-wilds of Darkness waving midnight-locks.
Mad war outbellows many devils damn'd.
Hell grows outrageous as a sea for prey.
King-majesty sat on his brow with ease.
And his life's day was one straight march to God.
An earth-wide army and a world of men.
A battle-driving Spirit consummate.
For Virtue's eye e'er looks on Victory.
Vengeance in midst bares his red arm of hell.
Her arrow's flight the coming-on of Death.
As ghosts of night from world-rejoicing Morn.
Be swords to fight the Battle of the Lord," etc.

These are but a few gems hastily culled from that casket of jewels—" The Closing Scene." Long extracts might be taken of surprising Beauty, Horror and Sublimity; but I have chosen to take single lines alone, in order to show the reader how much can be compassed by one far-sweeping thought. None but a genius God-inspired could have penned the lines above, "and unto airy Nothing gave a local habitation and a name."

S. T. BROOK.

INVOCATIONS.—The finest Invocations in the English language are Milton's, Pollok's, and Woodmansee's. Let us examine them a moment.

Milton's is classic and learned, but without its cadence, it would be mere prose. Harmony of numbers is one of the qualities of Poetry, but it is not Poesy herself; we want more than word-music, and prose in measure is contemptible doggerel. Destroy the rhythm of Milton's Invocation, and you make prose at once; but worse than all,—*it is not his own!* Both Virgil and Milton have stolen their Invocations from Homer; let us bring the Iliad and Paradise Lost side by side and see. I give a literal translation from the Iliad:

"Of Achilles deadly wrath, the source of many thousand woes to Greece, which sent countless souls of heroes down to Hell, and left their bodies to devouring dogs and birds,—sing Muse! Who of the Gods impelled them to contend? The son of Latona and of Jove. He it was, whose rage burnt hot against the king, fierce Contagion sent to all the host, and multitudes destroyed."

Now hear Milton:—"Of Man's first disobedience and the fruit of that forbidden tree, whose mortal taste brought death into the world, and all our woe—sing Heavenly Muse! Who first seduced them to that foul revolt? The infernal Serpent; he it was, whose guile, stirred up with envy and revenge, deceived the mother of mankind." Who can not see, that this Invocation is but the *adopted* child of old John Bull, even a step-son of the great father of Poets—Homer himself?

The rest of Milton's Invocation is taken from Scripture except the couplet:—

"I may assert eternal Providence
And justify the ways of God to man."

Two very beautiful lines indeed, and I know not from whom he stole them. Milton as far surpasses all Poets in plagiarism, as his great Epic does all the Poems in the English language.

Not so with Pollok,—he is no thief; all the gems he has are his own, and they are Legion. 'The Course of Time' is not so great a poem as 'Paradise Lost,' and far below the glory of 'The Iliad,' but it will do more good to the world, than both these mighty Epics together:—but to his Invocation.

As sure as 'Eternal Spirit' is 'God of Truth,' so sure Pollok has written tautology in the first, and nonsense in the second line of his immortal Poem. Things '*seem*' to men, but to 'God of Truth,'—all truths are truths. '*Thou*,' in the second line, makes his Invocation read thus:—"Eternal Spirit! God of truth! to whom all things seem as they are; Eternal Spirit! God of Truth! who of old,'—eight tautologous words in two lines! But let that pass; to show all his tautology would fill a volume.

Pollok is unclassical in some of his expressions, and frequently he seems not to know the power of words:—"Muse chanting loud in windy rhyme." The word "*windy*" is out of place; there is *correct* and *false* rhyme, but—"Muse chanting loud in windy rhyme," is a monstrosity, and belongs not to the tuneful Nine that on Parnassus dwelt.

In the following, Pollok reveals his greatness:—

"Hold my right hand, Almighty! and me teach
To strike the lyre, but seldom struck, to notes
Harmonious with the morning stars, and pure
As those by sainted bards and angels sung,
Which wake the echoes of eternity.'

This is to strike the lyre that will wake the echoes of Eternity. It excels all the Invocations written before Pollok's day. How fearfully bold is the thought:—"*Hold my right hand, Almighty!*" I know not its equal in any language. Indeed, the whole of his Invocation, save a few jumble of words, and confusion of ideas, is exceedingly beautiful, and it is excelled alone by the Invocation of "The Closing Scene," where no confusion is, but all is pure and classic as the Classics themselves. How divine is the opening of this Poem!

"First Cause of every cause—Almighty Cause!
Forever present, always Ancient One,—
The life of all, great Being's dawn and end—
All-making Lord—the All in All and Sire,
From everlasting to e'erlasting—God!
Incomprehensible and infinite—
The fullness of Immensity for aye!
To whom, the Heaven of Heavens is but a seat,
A footstool Earth, and Hell—a spark of fire!"

There is no finer address to Deity than this. Without such a God, all worlds would be

"A Speck of dust 'mid Chaos' deep profound,
A mote on bosom of Nonentity—
Too small a fiber for the scales of Nought!"

This reminds us of that heavenly Epic sung by the Divine Poet and Lawgiver:—

God said, "Let there be Light:" and there was LIGHT!

Where find such soul-devotion as in the following:—

"O, rise my soul! with holy Rapture rise
To adoration mute–astonishment!
With sacred awe and spirit-trembling breathe
Thy thoughts too hallow'd all for utterance,

In deep, dead-silence dumb with reverence
His name eternal musing—lost in Him!
This world from thine immortal pinions shake,
Shake imperfection—mix with Purities
Whose every thought 's a prayer and breath a psalm
And God their all in all eternally."

Woodmansee's Invocation, might with great propriety, have commenced with these lines:—

"Spirit of God! thou—Light Ineffable!
Brood o'er the dark of my chaotic mind
As "o'er the water's face" when Nature's self
Confusion lay the bosom of Old Night:—
With Glory's flame and Thy divinity
Illume me as Thou didst Creation then,
That rose complete to magnify Thy power—
Stupendous wonder grand to Angel-eye,
To mortal sight another Deity," etc.

This is full of glory as noonday. How Gabriel-like he talks with his "Almighty Cause," in the following:

"The Closing Scene, in wond'rous Visions wild
Give me to sing assisted by Thy power
T' sonorous note of tempest-melody,
Or deep-ton'd organ of Eternity
That smites the listless ear of hideous Ghosts
In Den of Night, and stuns the Wo-gnaw'd soul
Of Melancholy, wreck'd, in chamber damn'd."

What an awful Harp is here invoked! Is there an Invocation in any language that can compare with this? None that I know. Lo! how Angel-like comes his *Vision!* It far transcends Dante's, or any "attempted yet in prose or rhyme:—"

"When orient
To spirit-sight—all-seeing *Vision* came!
Her wing celestial plum'd, and to me gave
The Valley of the Shade of Death! Rolled up
The curtain dark of Doom. Mind's startled eye
Affrighted sore, drank in—Eternal Scenes!"

The Invocation of 'The Closing Scene," with great propriety, may be called a—***Psalm.*** Should an Apocrypha ever be added to the Psalms, this devout and sublime Invocation, will be—'The First Psalm;'—as all-worthy to end the divine songs of the sweet singer of Israel, as The Apocrypha to close the Old Testament. REV. M. C. C.

ON EULOGY.

[AN EXTRACT.]

In Book III of the Closing Scene, the Poet paints the full-length Portraits of many great personages, and I must own they are sketches of surpassing power,—all models of Eulogy to be studied in ages yet to come. Woodmansee puts the heroes of Antiquity into his crucible and seethes them to an essence, then gives us *the spirit of his hero.* Never was there more history in fewer lines; Cesar told not more in his celebrated letter:—"*Veni vidi vici*"—than our poet in the same space in his pen-Portraits—a volume to a thought! When I first read them, I wrote a very shy word, (almost a stranger on Earth) '*Perfection,*' on every one of them, and I have not called for my India-rubber yet. Every time I examine them I exclaim as Pilate did of Christ:—"I find no fault in them." Here is Eulogy in its perfection,—just in sentiment, original and far-sweeping in idea, and every thought a wreathe of glory glittering diamonds. Heretofore, Tacitus excelled all writers in Eulogy, but we had no perfect Model till Woodmansee wrote his third book of the Closing Scene. I would like to give long extracts here, but I must confine myself to mere items. Hear him talk of HOMER:—

"Fame's wonder and the Muse of Bards for aye,—
The household-god for soul of all the world!
Bright Glory's spire on temple of Renown—
His name is Glory's ornament and pride!
Alone in glory like the sun in heaven
Whose day-bright firmament admits no star:
Terrific rolleth on his thunder thoughts
And lightnings flash from every lay he sings,—
The Jove of Song! he lives a thunder-peal
In ear of Time till Earth shall be no more."

How beautifully he speaks of SAPPHO:

"Whose life a poem and pall a drama was.
Her harp Heaven-tuned to sweetest harmony
Eolian, and thoughts a thousand flowers!"

And England's great dramatist:

SHAKSPEARE! what diamonds sparkled in thy mind!
A mind-mint coining thought unthought before—
The head and heart of every age for aye!
Reflection's self sat mighty in his soul:
Illumined spirit, Genius unsurpass'd—
He look'd upon the other side of things!
The child of Nature and the Son of Song,—
Inspir'd song peal'd from his immortal harp
As psalm of Heaven by Angel-lyre awoke.
He oped the human heart to eye of man:
His Dramas are Daguerreotypes of Life,
And they map out great Nature like a chart—

Of Nature s own handwriting a fac-simile!"

What a day-bright picture this of MILTON:

"Singer divine and Angel of the Earth,
He touch'd his lyre and Eden bloom'd again—
More heaven in him than all his age beside!
Too great a light for Death-shades to eclipse
And vast a glory for a tomb to hide."

He says of KIRK WHITE:

"His songs are very fragments of his heart,
And speak divinely like an Angel's voice."

He says of the "WILEY ULYSSES:"

"His history a tale and life a romance!
"A galaxy of stars shall crown his brow,
And Earth's heart be his living monument."

He calls ACHILLES:

"That most terrible of men—
The dreadful breaker of the ranks of war!
Storm-sweeping hero furious as Death!
An army-routing god—thunderous as Heaven!
Immortals bled—the mighty were in dust
And fury of his vengeance kill'd remote."

Of ALEXANDER:

'Like Death, his spirit had a quenchless thirst;
His orphan-breeding sword made desolate;
His hero-felling arm was foe's despair,—
Oppose his might and vanish out of being!
He laid his hand upon the World's great heart
And made it beat in union with his:

He stamp'd his mark of conquest on mankind,
And they, and their possessions number'd his."

Of CÆSAR:

"That man-of-men of mighty daring made!
He knew not fear and never heard of flight,
The soul of Valor and the battle's life—
The fearful victor of a thousand fields!
World-conqueror—right hand of Victory,—
He hid in Valor's cloak Ambition's deeds.
Throne-born, by Valor king'd and all the gods:
The shining wonder 'bove Earth's greatness tower'd—
A living Mars and mortal Jupiter!"

He calls WALLACE:

Victory of Valor.
War's flame in bosom of his patriots—
The heart and soul of every hero's breast!
He, in the greatness of his glory, towered—
Outpouring of his strength was majesty;
Wond'rous to men the story of his might,
All greatness save great Wallace' self, excelling."

There is more history in the Eulogy on Bonaparte, than there is in Sir Walter Scott's ponderous and novel-life of the great hero, but I must omit it, to give a few lines on WASHINGTON:

'Earth's pride and more than king—
Heaven's chosen sent to set a Nation free.
His world wide throne the heart of all mankind.
Beloved of Freedom and the bless'd of Heaven,—
He was of sacred Freedom born, and drank
In Liberty with his own mother's milk—

His cradle-song the song of Liberty!
Renown of arms and ornament of Peace;
His country's savior and that country's love;
Lyre's voice, and odes of many cannons' mouths.
Great parallel to Piety and Worth;
Just, noble, brave—hero to God and man,—
One whom Religion's self delights to laud!
Heaven's own anointed and her God-inspired
Divinity of greatness, glory of renown!
His greatness, would with Glory's light halo
All-lustrous, diadem of Universe,
And virtue, to its throne add ornament!
His wonderous deeds exalteth Heroism,
And Honor's path's illum'd with his god-light.
Like his great Parent—God! he gave to men
Treasure divine, e'en—FREEDOM—LIBERTY,
And INDEPENDENCE crown'd Columbia's brow!"

Then follows Newton, Franklin, Howard, Ginghas Kahn, Nero, Maximin—all immortal Daguerreotypes, but I have no more room for extracts; let all purchase a copy and—"feast on marrow and fat things." The III Book is worth thrice the price paid for the volume. L. A. KESSLING.

THE CLOSING SCENE.

There is no page in this wonderful Poem, on which we might not write:—"Beautiful, or Elegant, or Grand,—Splendid, Magnificent, Picturesque, Sublime." In horrific sublimity, it has no parallel,—Dante's Inferno does not equal it. I study the Closing Scene, as I do the Revelation of St. John, to lose myself in the Eternal World, till I seem to stand within the gates of Heaven. All the books written in this age, would not make —'The Closing Scene.' REV. H. MARSTON.

EXTRACT.

Ossian's Sun and Moon have been the admiration of the world from the time they were penned till the present, and they both glowed alone in their glory till the Sun and Moon of the Closing Scene eclipsed them both. No sun, but the one God's own finger made, shines with the brilliance, or "walks the heavens" with majesty like the "day-eyed sun" that illumes the Fifth Book of our American Iliad. I know of no thoughts more classical, elegant, far-reaching and sublime, than the Sun, Moon and Stars of this wonderful Poem. Indeed, all the Vision of the Millennial glory, is an unequaled Panoramic glory, whose picturesque brilliance and surpassing magnificence, makes all other paintings and poems poor in the comparison. C. K.

MELODY OF POEMS.

[AN EXTRACT.]

The Closing Scene, is the most melodious poem in the English language, Pope's sing-song not excepted. Open the volume where you will, and scan the first page that meets your eye, and you will be convinced that it is harmony itself:—

"No Spring to wake her little infants up!
No Summer paints her blushings on the pink
And rose's cheek, or heavens the violet's lip;
Nor yellow Autumn breathes to ripe her fruit,
Or view her leafy honors fly the breeze,
But Winter reigns sole monarch of the year.

This is Poetry as well as Melody. There are no prosy expressions in The Closing Scene, so frequently met with in our greatest Poets. Hear Milton himself:—

"No wonder, fallen such a pernicious hight;"

Or this:—

"Burnt after them to the bottomless pit;"

Or,

"For still they knew, and ought to have still remember'd."

He that "hath music in his soul," let him scan these, and he will find—a brier-bush. Here Milton falls "a pernicious" depth; who would think of making poetry of "No wonder?" It is strange that classic Milton made use of this unclassical expression, and let it stand so—a running ulcer in his immortal Epic. There are no such ulcers in The Closing Scene—not one. Woodmansee has an ear, and taste as fine as his ear, and the melody of his 'Closing Scene,' is the voice of the Eolian Harp. J. C. KING.

THE CLOSING SCENE.

This great Poem is modeled out as Longinus would have modeled it—*sublimity itself.* Its imagery, description, language and thought, fill every rule laid down by the Greek Critic in his work—"ON THE SUBLIME."

The Scene, is laid in Oblivion,—and what a horrific Panorama it spreads out to our view!

"On Horror's head horrors accumulate."

Dante's Inferno nor Milton's Hell, does not equal it. All is horridly majestic, and each Description is painted out life-size, and is as Homer would have painted it—simple in word and powerful in effect. Woodmansee is not satisfied with the common-place trash of "To-day," but he wisely goes back to classic Antiquity and models his Poem after the old immortal Bards. He has studied Homer with great care, and drank in the spirit of his master till we feel the great father of Poetry lives again, and we are persuaded that both Justice and Truth must call the author of The Closing Scene, the '*Christian Melesigenes.*'

If he finish his last Six Books, complete and perfect as he has done the six already given to the world, and they all make one complete whole, The Closing Scene will be a great

National work, such as America has been in travail to bring forth from her womanhood, and it will crown its Author emphatically—the Homer of America. There is nothing our Literature wants more than such a work; it would be a sun to day her night that never yet has known a morn; it would give the New World character and notoriety abroad,—wreath her brow with brighter glories, and send her name further than many Presidents.

If there is anything that can make a great nation forever a debtor,—forever too poor to pay, it is such a work. Could Greece have paid her Homer for writing the Iliad?

"Homer is gone; and where is Jove? and where
The rival cities seven? His song outlives
Time, tower and god—all that then *was* save Heaven."

My prayer goes up morning and evening, that the Author may live to complete 'The Closing Scene,' and feel the Laurel crown a weight of glory on his brow. CLIO.

THE NEW POEM.

Chance threw in my way—The Closing Scene, a Poem printed at the Methodist Book Concern in 1857. I had not heard of the book before, and seeing where it was published, I thought to myself,—'something prosy, of course.' I opened it near the middle, and thought I could scan it to the end, e'er the opiate would give me to the lap of Dreams. What was my surprise! Reader, did you ever sleep in the open air, and awake at midnight to find all the stars of heaven laughing down in your face? If you did, and have a soul in your body, you can tell how I felt while reading the 217th page of The Closing Scene. Stars of the first magnitude rushed blazingly to view from every thought I met, till my very soul was illumed by the glory of 'The Closing Scene.' I purchased a copy, and I have read it over and over again, and at every reading, still new glories open to my view. I study it—line by line as I do the mysteries of Revelation, "feasting on marrow and fat things. What beautiful descriptions! How picturesque! What invention! What power of language and originality of thought! What fire, grandeur and awful sublimity!

"On Horror's head horrors accumulate!"

and yet as beautiful as May-morning!

B. S. LONG,
Author of "Alethea."

OUR REVIEW.

"America's the land
Where Genius sickens and where Fancy dies."

America has produced—An Ode to Shakspeare, Marco Bozzaris and Parrhasius, and diamonds they all are,—all perfect little gems; but gems are little trifles after all. They will not stand up as beacon-lights in the dark night of Futurity,and noon all Nations as a summer's sun, and give Fame's crown of glory to Columbia's brow. We have produced no National Work—no Epic that hallows Poetry as a thing from God,—an Inspiration sent like a flaming comet to win a wild-eyed gaze from all the world, and splendor up the night of dim Futurity.

I grant, "The Columbiad," has books complete, but 12 books don't make an Epic,—"clapt hodge-podge together, they don't make a tree." 'Tis *quality* we want, not *quantity*. A great deal of a dull thing,is a great deal too much. The Columbiad has the rhyme, but not the poetry, pathos, fire, sublimity, invention and genius of an Epic Poem; and therefore, it lays its weight of dullness on the shelf—an intolerable great bore.

"America's the land
Where Genius sickens and where Fancy dies."

This hackneyed old slur has filled the mouth of England from time immemorial, and haunted

"The land of the free and the home of the brave,"

like an Evil Genius; the very sound, more hateful to our ears than the hoot of an owl,—and hateful, alas! because it is too true. Shall this despised old Death's head grin out on our happy America from infancy till she is graved? If so, I care not how soon her grave is dug. All countries have their National Poems but America:—O, mother! why art thou so long barren?

But, where shall our Homer be born? Where should he be but in the far West? E'en, in the wilderness, where Fashion, Vanity and Luxury shall not corrupt the man, enfeeble the soul—fetter and enslave the immortal Mind. Yes, let him be born in the West, where Nature in her nakedness is seen, and where Fancy has room to spread her wing, and Mind expand huge as a Prairie. Such alone shall write our Epic, and not

"A lisping, curl'd gallant, with words in mouth
Soft as his mother's milk," and band-box in
A city!

Yes, in the West, he is ALREADY BORN, and our Iliad—ALREADY WRITTEN. Reader, be not surprised at this, but keep your astonishment to wonder with 'exceeding great wonder' when I tell you—THAT ILIAD LIES ON THE SHELF UNCALLED FOR AND UNREAD! Thus Greece served her Homer and England her Milton long as they lived! Who shall be our Addison to bring the Milton of America from this night of Ignorance, and introduce him to the world—a God-send dropped from Heaven? We have long agonized for a living American Poem; it is published, and the first Edition—unsold. It is an anomaly, that sensible and good men will laud to the skies, the heart-corrupting, mind-enfeebling common-place of Dickens, Bulwer, Sue and Scott, while the true works of Genius that bear the stamp of Immortality in every thought—lay on the shelf! There is more splendor of thought and originality, in one page of 'The Closing Scene' than all the trash Eugene Sue ever penned, and yet 'The Mysteries of Paris' had a world-wide sale,—

"O, judgment! thou art fled to brutish beasts
And men have lost their reason!"

The Closing Scene is an Epic, and the great Battle fought, is not to gain the hand of a fickle woman, as is the case of The Æneid, nor by a few cowardly Trojans and outrageous Grecians as found in the Iliad, but it is for the conquest not only of Earth but great Being's self, climaxed with "The wreck of matter and the crush of worlds." So we see, the *Scene* of this wonderful Poem, infinitely transcends all the Epic poems put together; and not only so, but it is impossible for the imagination of man to conceive a greater scene than the one laid in this sublime Epic; all greatness is swallowed up therein—beyond Imagination itself!

The *Characters*, too, are vast and awful as the sublime and terrible scene,—*God and Man; Life and Death; Time and Eternity.* The rankling critic, may be disposed to snarl because some of the characters are Allegorical; but he must swallow his own venom, for The Closing Scene is a *Vision;* and in Vision's Vale, *all is allegory.* Grim Death (a character true to the nature of things) is the all-prevailing Hero of the Poem, and not only drives Gog and Magog to a great Epic Battle, but he has his dart barbed for Mortality herself. What a dreadful character is the Grim Death of The Closing Scene! He stands alone—the King of Terrors with every Horror crowned. Homer, Virgil and Dante's heroes, infernals and spirit damned, are shadows to Woodmansee's Hell-begotten monster—Death.

His direful form of famine looks disease
And battle forth with pestilence and wo,
Whiles Dissolution gurgles from his throat.
Destruction-arm'd and Terror-clad he stands
A statued Horror—Fate is in his look!
His eye the fiery lightning's sheeted flame,
And arm the lowering thunder's desperate might.
His laboring brain a carnage-house of wo
Haunted and fed by fury of his soul,—

Death-dooms are seen wide-written on his face!
Diseases thicken 'round about him grim;
Plague, Pestilence, in fatal shadow stand,
And 'hind him Desolation and Despair
Spread their domain thro' Chaos down to Hell.
A sight so fell that Darkness midnights 'round,
Ghosts shriek, and Echo bellows out—'GRIM DEATH!'

Milton's Satan has been by critics pronounced the sublimest character portrayed by the Poets. Let us bring these awful Heroes side by side, and look at them. Milton thus describes Satan:—

Thus Satan, talking to his nearest mate,
With head uplift the wave, and eyes
That sparkling blazed; his other parts besides
Prone on the flood, extended long and large,
Lay floating many a rood; in bulk as huge
As whom the fables name of monstrous size,
Titanian, or Earth-born that warr'd on Jove;
Briareus, or Typhon, whom the den
By ancient Tarsus held; or that sea-beast—
Leviathan, which God of all his works
Created hugest that swim the ocean stream:
Him, haply, slumbering on the Norway foam
The pilot of some small night-founder'd skiff,
Deeming some island, oft, as seamen tell,
With fixed anchor in his scaly rind,
Moors by his side under the lee, while night
Invests the sea, and wish'd-for morn delays:
So stretch'd out huge in length the arch-fiend lay.

This is Milton's description of Satan; now for Woodmansee's Grim Death:—

The world's Goliaths vast and Sampsons strong
To him compared contemptuous pigmies are,—
More mighty than Xerxes five millions arm'd!
Towery his form! A promontory seem'd
That frowns to scorn old Ocean's lashing Tides
And storm-begotten children of the Deep,—
Colossus shading half Oblivion!
His giant shoulders fearful in their strength
Hung massy-huge and broad and round, and might
At will upheave from fixed foundations firm
The Apennines with all their weight of woods.
His arm of strength, too, wield a thousand oaks,
Or hurl to sky, or snap them all in twain
As boy the cane that dangles at his side.
His hand of bone in its fell grasp of death,
Pluck Gibraltar from rock-rooted base,
And fling afar to middle of the sea.
His face of storm look'd devastation wide
And age and ruin gnawed by Sin and Wo—
Abaddon-deadly hollow of his jaw!
Diseases-millioned, cavern'd in his grin.
His eyes, out flaming anger's wasteful fires,
Like baleful comets from their dreadful orbs
Roll'd fearful wilds of emptiness remote.
Upon his brow dread Vengeance hung and all
The frowns of Night. His Hell-fill'd bosom's core
Like Hecla burn'd with its infernal stores—
Satanic-soul a-struggle to devour!

A raging Ruin and all-smiting Curse,
And vast Oblivion 'neath his fury shook.

Nothing can be more natural than this description; each comparison and figure is familiar to every reader, and yet how terrific and sublime he has made Grim Death! To me, it has no equal. Woodmansee goes not to Mythology to idolatrize his Holy Harp like Milton has done, to drag from that heathen night of shadows, a fabled Typhon, that even the learned know very little about, and that little to be—*all a lie!* Our young Homer measures his hero by square-and-compass accuracy that boys can understand, while Milton measures his to show the world—he has read a little Latin and some Greek. But Milton's great fault is, in comparing Satan to a—BEAST! A beast that surpasses all belief, and out-fables fable. What a ridiculous figure for him "whose form had not yet lost all its original brightness," to so stretch himself out like a "sea-beast" till a Pilot mistook him for "some island," and "anchor'd in his scaly rind—moored by his side all night—under the lee."

But I must close. I will review 'The Closing Scene,' Book by Book, when the Lord gives me better health. No author thinks more like Homer than Woodmansee; all his descriptions breathe forth the true spirit of the Epic.

REV. H. S. SELLMAN.

www.ingramcontent.com/pod-product-compliance
Lightning Source LLC
LaVergne TN
LVHW021402110826
845150LV00007B/1750